Diabetic Diet Cookbook:

Delicious Recipes for Every Day, that Promote Better Health, Including 30-Day Meal Plan & Preparation Tips

By Tori Jones

Disclaimer:

My dear friend! I am happy you've chosen this cookbook as a companion in your journey toward healthier, diabetes-friendly meals. Every recipe here has been lovingly crafted to support balanced blood sugar levels and delicious, nutritious eating.

However, a little reminder: everyone's health is unique, and what works well for one person may not be perfect for another. These recipes are designed as general guidelines rather than personalized medical advice. Before diving in, especially if you have specific dietary needs or health concerns, it's a good idea to consult your healthcare provider to ensure these meals are suitable for you.

I am here to inspire, but you're the expert on you! Enjoy these dishes, listen to your body, and savor every bite on your journey to wellness.

With best wishes,

Tori Jones

Table of Contents

Introduction: A Delicious Path to Better Health

Welcome to your journey towards a healthier, more vibrant life! Managing diabetes or prediabetes doesn't mean sacrificing the joy of eating. In fact, with the proper guidance and recipes, you can indulge in flavorful meals while taking control of your health. This cookbook was created to empower you to savor each bite while making informed, mindful choices.

Whether you're newly diagnosed, supporting a loved one, or simply seeking to elevate your overall well-being, you'll find a treasure chest of easy, delicious, and nutritious recipes here that cater to your needs. From hearty, energizing breakfasts to satisfying dinners and guilt-free desserts that will delight your taste buds, each recipe is crafted with particular attention to stabilizing blood sugar levels without compromising flavor.

You'll discover an abundance of meals designed to be rich in fiber, lean proteins, healthy fats, and low-glycemic carbohydrates. These balanced options are good for you and effortlessly easy to prepare, featuring wholesome ingredients easily found at your local grocery store. I aim to seamlessly weave healthier eating into your everyday life, ensuring it feels effortless and enjoyable.

In addition to scrumptious recipes, this cookbook offers a wealth of valuable resources, including handy tips on meal planning, portion control, and essential nutritional guidelines—all designed to make managing diabetes less daunting and more fulfilling. It's not just about learning to eat right; it's about embracing a lifestyle that empowers you to live well.

Join us as we embark on this delicious journey together, savoring the pleasure of every meal while enhancing your health, one bite at a time. Your path to thriving health starts here—let's make it a flavorful adventure you won't want to miss!

Chapter 1: Understanding Diabetes and Nutrition

Diabetes mellitus is a chronic metabolic disorder characterized by hyperglycemia resulting from defects in insulin secretion, insulin action, or both. Understanding diabetes is crucial for effective management and prevention of complications. The two primary forms of diabetes are Type 1 and Type 2, along with a condition known as prediabetes, each with distinct pathophysiological mechanisms and implications for treatment.

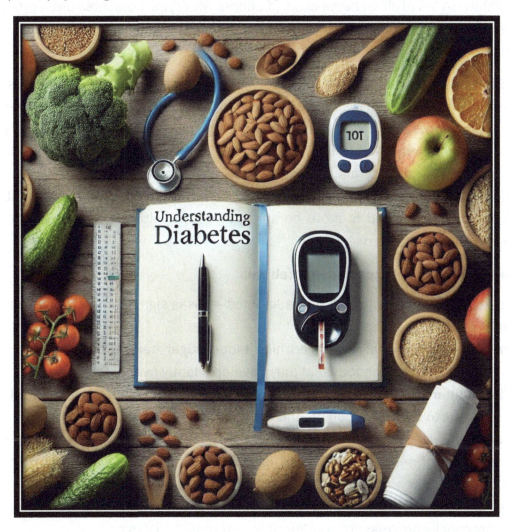

Prediabetes is a condition that occurs when blood glucose levels are higher than usual but not yet high enough to be classified as Type 2 diabetes. It is often seen as a critical warning sign indicating an increased risk of developing Type 2 diabetes, heart disease, and stroke. Individuals with prediabetes may be asymptomatic, but risk factors include obesity, physical inactivity, a sedentary lifestyle, and a family history of diabetes.

Early intervention through lifestyle modifications such as weight loss, dietary changes, and increased physical activity can significantly lower the risk of progressing to Type 2 diabetes.

Studies show that structured lifestyle interventions can delay or even prevent the onset of diabetes in those with prediabetes.

Type 1 Diabetes (T1D) is an autoimmune condition wherein the immune system erroneously attacks and destroys the insulin-producing beta cells in the pancreas. This results in absolute insulin deficiency, necessitating lifelong exogenous insulin therapy to manage blood glucose levels. Typically diagnosed in children and young adults, T1D accounts for approximately 5-10% of all diabetes cases. Patients with Type 1 diabetes often present with classic symptoms such as polyuria (excessive urination), polydipsia (increased thirst), and unexplained weight loss.

Type 2 Diabetes In contrast, Type 2 diabetes (T2D) primarily involves insulin resistance, where the body's cells do not respond effectively to insulin, combined with a relative insulin deficiency over time. T2D is associated mainly with lifestyle factors such as obesity, physical inactivity, and poor dietary habits. It often develops gradually and can go unnoticed for years, leading to chronic hyperglycemia. Patients with Type 2 diabetes may experience symptoms like those of T1D, but they are often less pronounced. T2D typically accounts for about 90-95% of diabetes cases and is more common in adults, although its incidence among children and adolescents is rising.

The Health Risks of Diabetes and Prediabetes

Diabetes—whether Type 1, Type 2, or prediabetes—poses significant risks to health due to its potential for serious complications:

1. **Chronic Hyperglycemia:** Prolonged high blood sugar can damage vital organs and systems, leading to complications that may develop silently over time.

2. **Cardiovascular Disease:** Diabetes increases the risk of heart attacks, strokes, and hypertension due to the promotion of atherosclerosis, which restricts blood flow.

3. **Neuropathy:** High glucose levels can cause diabetic neuropathy, resulting in pain, tingling, and loss of sensation in the extremities, increasing the risk of foot ulcers and amputations.

4. **Kidney Damage:** Diabetic nephropathy can occur as blood sugar damages kidney function, potentially progressing to kidney failure requiring dialysis.

5. **Eye Complications:** Diabetic retinopathy can lead to vision impairment and blindness due to damage to the blood vessels in the retina.

6. **Increased Risk of Infections:** Elevated blood sugar levels can weaken the immune system, making it harder to fight infections.

7. **Mental Health Challenges:** Managing diabetes can lead to psychological stress, anxiety, and depression, impacting overall quality of life.

8. **Complications of Prediabetes:** Prediabetes signals an increased risk of developing Type 2 diabetes and its complications, necessitating early lifestyle interventions.

Understanding the risks associated with diabetes and prediabetes is crucial for effective management. Adopting a balanced diet, engaging in regular physical activity, and monitoring blood glucose levels can mitigate these dangers and enhance overall health.

The Role of Nutrition and Lifestyle Modification.

"You are what you eat," a quote attributed to French author Jean Anthelme Brillat-Savarin in 1826, reflects a powerful truth: the food we consume directly impacts our health and well-being. This is particularly true when it comes to managing diabetes and prediabetes.

Regardless of the type of diabetes or prediabetes, the importance of nutrition in glycemic control cannot be overstated. A diet rich in low-glycemic index foods, fiber, lean proteins, and healthy fats is integral to managing blood glucose levels. High-fiber foods, such as whole grains, legumes, fruits, and vegetables, improve glycemic control and promote satiety.

Moreover, regular physical activity can enhance insulin sensitivity and aid in weight management. It is recommended that individuals at risk of prediabetes and those with diabetes engage in at least 150 minutes of moderate-intensity aerobic exercise each week and resistance training to build muscle mass and promote metabolic health.

Balancing Carbohydrates, Proteins, and Fats

1. Carbohydrates: Your Energy Source Carbohydrates often get a bad rap in the context of diabetes, but they really can be your friend when chosen wisely. They are the body's primary energy source, fueling your physical and mental activities.

Complex Carbohydrates: Embrace whole, unprocessed sources such as whole grains (like brown rice, quinoa, and oats), legumes, fruits, and a rainbow of vegetables. These foods are fiber-rich, promoting a slower release of glucose into the bloodstream. Think of them as the steady friends who help you maintain energy throughout your day.

Simple Carbohydrates: These are found in sugary snacks and processed foods; while they may offer a quick energy boost, they can lead to rapid spikes in blood sugar. Limiting these foods and opting for more wholesome alternatives can create a more stable foundation for your health.

2. Proteins: The Building Blocks of Your Wellness. Protein is essential for your body, playing a pivotal role in repairing tissues and helping you feel satisfied. Including lean proteins in your meals is an integral part of managing diabetes.

Lean Protein Sources: Consider incorporating skinless poultry, fish, legumes, eggs, and low-fat dairy. These proteins can help balance blood sugar and promote satiety, making you feel fuller. An excellent way to savor protein is to enjoy it as part of a meal you love—consider it a nourishing hug for your body.

3. Healthy Fats: Nurturing Your Body Healthy fats are critical to a well-rounded diet. They provide essential fatty acids and aid in absorbing fat-soluble vitamins, all while supporting your brain function, hormone balance, and heart health.

Unsaturated Fats: Source your fats from avocados, nuts, seeds, and olive oil. These healthy options enhance the flavor of your meals and contribute to your overall well-being. Remember, moderation is vital, so indulge mindfully in these nutrient-dense foods that satisfy your meals.

Understanding Glycemic Index and Glycemic Load

1. Glycemic Index (GI): A Helpful Guide The glycemic index is a valuable tool for understanding how different foods impact blood sugar levels. Foods are ranked based on their ability to raise blood glucose, enabling you to make informed choices.

Low GI Foods: Foods categorized as low (55 or less) are your best allies for maintaining stable blood sugar levels. These include most fruits, whole grains, legumes, and non-starchy vegetables—nourishing options that provide lasting energy.

Moderate to High GI Foods: Foods with higher GI scores provide quick energy but can lead to rapid blood sugar spikes. While it's okay to enjoy these occasionally, being aware of them will help you choose more stable options most of the time.

2. Glycemic Load (GL): A Comprehensive Perspective Glycemic Load considers both the GI and the quantity of carbohydrates in a serving size, offering a fuller understanding of how food may impact your blood sugar:

Calculating Glycemic Load: $$\text{GL} = \left(\text{GI} \times \text{grams of carbohydrate in a serving}\right) / 100$$ This calculation allows you to focus on not just the type of carbohydrate, but the practical effect it might have in your meals.

Putting It All Together

Creating balanced meals is vital in managing diabetes effectively and supports your overall health and well-being. Here are some supportive tips to help guide your meal planning:

Plate Method: Visualize your plate: half-filled with colorful, non-starchy vegetables, a quarter with lean protein, and a quarter with whole grains or high-fiber carbohydrates. This simple guideline can help you build a nutritious meal with ease.

Pairing Foods for Stability: Combine carbohydrates with proteins and healthy fats to help slow digestion and minimize blood sugar spikes. For example, enjoy whole-grain toast topped with creamy avocado and a poached egg—a treat that satisfies both your taste buds and your nutritional needs.

Mindful Portion Sizes: Being mindful of portion sizes for carbohydrates can prevent unwanted spikes in blood glucose. Smaller plates can naturally help control portions, creating a more satisfying meal experience.

In conclusion, by embracing the essential roles of carbohydrates, proteins, and fats and understanding glycemic index and load, you can make informed dietary choices supporting your health journey. This balanced approach helps maintain stable blood glucose levels and encourages you to enjoy the pleasures of cooking and eating.

Eating well is not simply about restrictions; it's about nourishing your body with wholesome foods that fuel your life. Embrace each meal as an opportunity to explore new flavors, try creative recipes, and celebrate your efforts in managing diabetes.

Remember, you are not alone on this journey. There is a vibrant community of individuals who are also embracing healthier choices. By sharing experiences and learning from each other, you can find inspiration and motivation to make sustainable changes.

With the proper knowledge and tools, every meal can be a step towards better health and greater enjoyment of life. Let the journey unfold, savor every bite, and feel empowered as you make choices that support your well-being!

Goals of the Cookbook

Welcome to a transformative culinary experience designed specifically for those navigating the path of diabetes management. The goals of this cookbook extend beyond mere recipes; they encompass a holistic approach to nurturing your health and empowering you to enjoy every meal without compromise. As you embark on this journey, I want to ensure you understand what this cookbook aims to achieve and how it can serve as your trusted companion.

1. Empowerment Through Knowledge

One of the primary goals of this cookbook is to empower you with knowledge about diabetes, nutrition, and the role food plays in your health. I strive to demystify the dietary aspects of managing diabetes, providing you with insights into macronutrients, glycemic index, and portion control. With this knowledge, you can confidently approach your meals, making informed choices that align with your health goals.

2. Celebrating Flavorful Nutrition

Living with diabetes doesn't mean sacrificing flavor. My goal is to redefine the way you perceive healthy eating. This cookbook showcases diverse, delicious recipes that celebrate wholesome ingredients, ensuring that each meal is nutritious and enjoyable. I believe that good food should be a source of joy. By exploring various cuisines and flavors, you'll discover that healthy eating can be a satisfying and pleasurable experience.

3. Practical and Accessible Solutions

I understand that busy lives often make it challenging to maintain healthy eating habits. This cookbook aims to provide practical solutions for meal planning and preparation, making it easier for you to incorporate nutritious meals into your daily routine. With simple ingredients, straightforward instructions, and time-saving tips, you can create wholesome dishes without spending hours in the kitchen. I want to show you that healthy cooking can be easy and rewarding.

4. Building a Supportive Community

Another goal of this cookbook is to foster community and support among individuals managing diabetes. By sharing recipes, tips, and experiences, I aim to create a space where you can connect with others who share similar challenges and triumphs. Whether through family meals, sharing dishes with friends, or engaging in online discussions, we encourage you to build connections that enrich your journey.

5. Inspiring a Healthier Lifestyle

More than just a collection of recipes, this cookbook is a stepping stone towards a healthier lifestyle. I encourage you to embrace the journey of self-care, intuition, and personal growth. Each recipe is designed to inspire you to explore new foods, develop culinary skills, and cultivate a deep appreciation for the nourishment that comes from balanced eating.

6. Cultivating Mindfulness and Balance

Finally, my goal is to instill a sense of mindfulness around food. I want to remind you to savor each bite, appreciate the flavors, and be present during your meals. Mindful eating can increase satisfaction, helping you listen to your body's cues and fostering a healthier relationship with food. By focusing on balance, you can navigate your dietary choices to honor your health and enjoyment of life.

As you embark on this culinary adventure within the pages of this cookbook, remember that your goals and aspirations for better health are just as important as the recipes you'll explore. Each meal you prepare allows you to nurture your body, share joy with loved ones, and take strides toward optimal health. Let's embrace this journey with enthusiasm, curiosity, and a commitment to living our best lives—one delicious meal at a time.

Chapter 2: Meal Preparation for Success

Pantry Essentials: Stock Your Kitchen with the Right Ingredients

Creating a well-stocked pantry is essential to managing diabetes effectively and embracing a healthier lifestyle. This chapter aims to guide you in selecting the right ingredients that support balanced eating while providing convenience and variety. By understanding each food group's importance and role in blood sugar management, you can confidently empower yourself to navigate your culinary journey.

1. Whole Grains: Your Foundation

Whole grains are rich in fiber, vitamins, and minerals, making them a cornerstone of a healthy diet for individuals with diabetes. Unlike refined grains, which can cause rapid spikes in blood sugar, whole grains digest slowly, promoting steady energy levels.

Essential Whole Grains to Stock:

Brown Rice: A nutritious alternative to white rice; it provides more fiber and nutrients.

Quinoa: A complete protein and gluten-free option, quinoa is versatile for salads, bowls, or sides.

Oats: Rolled or steel-cut oats are perfect for hearty breakfasts and can be used in baking.

Whole Wheat Pasta: Offers more fiber than regular pasta, helping to keep you full and satisfied.

Barley: A fiber-rich grain that works well in soups and salads.

2. Legumes: Nutrient-Packed Powerhouses

Legumes are an excellent source of protein, fiber, and essential nutrients. They help stabilize blood sugar levels and keep you full longer, making them an intelligent choice for meal planning.

Must-Have Legumes:

Beans: Black beans, kidney beans, pinto beans, and cannellini beans are great options for salads, stews, and dips.

Lentils: High in protein and fiber, lentils cook quickly and are perfect for soups and salads.

Chickpeas: These versatile legumes can be used in salads, roasted for snacks, or blended into hummus.

3. Healthy Fats: Nourishing Your Body

Incorporating healthy fats into your diet can help improve heart health and provide sustained energy. Focus on unsaturated fats, which can enhance your culinary creations and promote overall well-being.

Healthy Fats to Include:

Olive Oil: A staple in Mediterranean diets, olive oil is perfect for dressings and cooking.

Avocados: Packed with monounsaturated fats and fiber, they add creaminess to salads and spreads.

Egg yolk: Contains the bulk of an egg's iron, folate, and vitamins. The yolks also contain two nutrients—lutein and zeaxanthin—that support eye and brain health.

Nuts and Seeds: Almonds, walnuts, chia seeds, and flaxseeds provide healthy fats, fiber, and protein.

4. Fresh and Frozen Produce: Vibrant and Nutritious

Fruits and vegetables are vital for a balanced diet, offering a wealth of vitamins, minerals, and antioxidants. They support overall health and help regulate blood sugar levels when consumed in moderation.

Essential Produce to Keep:

Non-Starchy Vegetables: Leafy greens, bell peppers, broccoli, zucchini, and cauliflower are nutrient-dense and low in carbohydrates.

Fruits: Berries, apples, and citrus fruits are lower in sugar and packed with fiber; keep them whole to benefit from their natural sweetness.

Herbs and Spices: Fresh or dried herbs like basil, oregano, cilantro, and spices like cinnamon and turmeric can enhance flavor without adding sugar or salt.

5. Dairy and Dairy Alternatives: Calcium and Beyond

Dairy products are essential sources of calcium and protein, and many options are available for those with lactose intolerance or preferences for plant-based diets.

Dairy Essentials:
Low-Fat or Fat-Free Milk: Choose options without added sugars for a healthy beverage or ingredient.

Greek Yogurt: Higher in protein and lower in sugar, it can be enjoyed as a snack, in smoothies, or as a base for dressings.

Cottage Cheese: A low-fat option that provides protein and works well in sweet and savory dishes.

Dairy Alternatives:
Unsweetened Almond or Soy Milk: Alternative options without added sugars that can be used in cooking, baking, or smoothies.

6. Pantry Staples: Versatile Essentials

In addition to the core food groups, having suitable pantry staples on hand will enhance your cooking and make meal preparation easier.

Key Pantry Staples:
Low-Sodium Broth: Use chicken, vegetables, or beef broth as a base for soups and stews.

Canned Tomatoes: Packed with flavor and nutrients, canned tomatoes are essential for sauces and soups.

Whole Grain Flours: Consider whole wheat flour, almond flour, or oat flour for healthier baking options.

Vinegar: Apple cider and balsamic vinegar are great for dressings and marinades.

Condiments and Sauces: Choose low-sugar and low-sodium options for ketchup, mustard, and soy sauce. These can enhance flavors without overwhelming your meals with unwanted sugars and salts.

Sweeteners: Opt for natural, low-calorie sweeteners such as stevia, erythritol, or monk fruit. These alternatives can satisfy your sweet tooth without causing spikes in blood sugar.

Cereals: Look for whole grain or bran cereals that are low in sugar and high in fiber. These can serve as a nutritious breakfast or snack option.

7. Planning Your Pantry

Building a well-stocked pantry is not just about ingredients; it's about creating a space that supports your health goals. Here are some tips for effective planning:

Organize by Categories: Arrange your items in categories (grains, legumes, proteins, spices) to make finding ingredients easier and to help you track what you have on hand.

Check Expiry Dates: Regularly review your pantry and remove items past their expiration date. This helps keep your space organized and ensures you cook with fresh ingredients.

Rotate Stock: Place newer items at the back of the pantry and older items in front; this ensures that you use ingredients before expiration.

Make a Grocery List: As you become familiar with your pantry essentials, create a grocery list to replenish items as needed. Planning will help you avoid impulse purchases and stick to healthy choices.

Stocking your pantry with the right ingredients lays the groundwork for a successful journey toward managing diabetes. Each ingredient serves a purpose, helping you to prepare wholesome and satisfying meals that support your health and well-being.

Remember, your pantry is more than just a collection of foods; it's a sanctuary for your health. With a focus on whole grains, legumes, healthy fats, fresh produce, dairy, and versatile staples, you can embrace the joy of cooking and the pleasure of nutritious eating.

As you fill your kitchen with these essential ingredients, you'll find that preparing diabetic-friendly meals becomes a joyous and creative process. Let your pantry inspire you to explore new recipes, try different combinations, and enjoy the delicious bounty of healthy living!

Meal Planning & Prep Tips: Simplifying Your Cooking While Keeping Meals Enjoyable

Embarking on your journey of managing diabetes doesn't have to be overwhelming or monotonous. In fact, with a little organization and creativity, meal planning and preparation can be a fulfilling and enjoyable experience. This chapter offers unique strategies to help you streamline your cooking process, make the most of your ingredients, and explore new recipes—all while ensuring your meals remain delicious and satisfying.

1. The Power of Planning

Set Aside Time for Meal Planning Carving out dedicated time each week to plan your meals can transform your culinary experience. Whether it's Sunday afternoon or a quiet weekday evening, use this time to brainstorm, create, and explore new ideas. This is your moment to reflect on what foods inspire you and how to incorporate them into your diet.

Create a Flexible Meal Framework Instead of rigidly planning every meal, develop a flexible framework. Choose a theme for each meal (e.g., Meatless Mondays, Taco Tuesdays, Soup Sundays) to simplify decisions while allowing for creativity. This approach helps you rotate ideas without feeling restricted, making meal planning something you look forward to each week.

2. Smart Shopping

Craft a Detailed Grocery List Once your meals are planned, create a comprehensive grocery list based on your menu. Organize your list by food categories (produce, proteins, grains, etc.) to make shopping more efficient and ensure you don't forget critical ingredients. This saves time in the store and helps you resist impulse purchases that may not align with your health goals.

Embrace Seasonal Produce. Incorporating seasonal fruits and vegetables into your meals can be a delightful way to enjoy freshness and variety. Seasonal produce often comes at a better price and boasts peak flavor. Visit local farmers' markets or grocery stores to discover what's in season and let it inspire your dishes.

3. Meal Prep Made Easy

Batch Cooking: The Secret Weapon Batch cooking is a game changer that simplifies your weekly cooking. Designate one day a week to prepare more significant portions of staple ingredients, such as grains, proteins, and roasted vegetables. Store these components in airtight containers in the refrigerator, allowing you to mix and match them easily for quick meals throughout the week.

For example, cook a big batch of quinoa, grill a few chicken breasts, and roast a medley of veggies. You can create different meals by pairing them differently daily, such as a quinoa salad, chicken wraps, and a nourishing grain bowl.

Pre-portion Snacks and Meals Consider pre-portioning snacks and meals into individual servings. Use small containers or Ziplock bags to divide nuts, cut-up veggies, yogurt, or homemade granola. This saves time when hunger strikes and ensures you have nutritious options readily available, reducing the likelihood of reaching for high-sugar snacks.

4. Cook Smart, Enjoy

Utilize One-Pot and Sheet-Pan Recipes Simplify cooking and reduce cleanup by embracing one-pot and sheet-pan recipes. These methods allow you to prepare a complete meal with minimal effort. For instance, toss chicken, vegetables, and spices onto a sheet pan, roast, and enjoy a wholesome dinner without multiple pots and pans.

Incorporate Leftovers Creatively Transform leftovers into new meals! Get creative by repurposing proteins or grains into different dishes. For example, leftover grilled chicken can become an ingredient in stir-fries, salads, or wraps. This not only minimizes food waste but also keeps meals interesting.

Explore Freezer-Friendly Meals Make the most of your cooking efforts by preparing freezer-friendly meals. Soups, stews, and casseroles can be made in larger quantities and frozen in portions for later use. You can thaw and reheat on busy days, ensuring you always have healthy options.

5. Make It Fun

Involve Family and Friends. Cooking can be a social activity! Invite family members or friends to join you in preparing meals. Involving others in the process can make cooking more enjoyable and provide opportunities to share ideas and learn new techniques.

Discover New Recipes Together Regularly explore new recipes that excite you. Set aside time to browse cookbooks or online platforms for diabetic-friendly recipes. Experimentation can keep meals fresh and enhance your culinary skills, so don't hesitate to try cuisines that pique your curiosity.

Celebrate Your Achievements As you incorporate these meal planning tips into your routine, take a moment to celebrate your progress. Acknowledge the effort you put into cooking and relish its positive impact on your health and well-being. Establish small rewards for yourself as you reach milestones, whether trying a new recipe or consistently planning meals for a month.

Effective meal planning and preparation are essential tools for managing diabetes while maintaining enjoyment in the kitchen. By implementing these strategies, you can simplify your cooking.

Breakfast: Energizing meals to start your day.

Berry Almond Overnight Oats

Prep time: 10 min	Chilling time: 4 hours (or overnight)	Serves: 2

Ingredients:

Base Ingredients:

1 cup unsweetened almond milk (or any other low-carb milk option)

1/2 cup rolled oats (preferably old-fashioned, as they are less processed)

1/2 cup non-fat Greek yogurt

one tablespoon of chia seeds (optional for added fiber)

one tablespoon of almond butter or 1 oz of almonds, chopped (for healthy fats)

Berry Mixture:

1/2 cup mixed berries (such as blueberries, strawberries, or raspberries) (fresh or frozen)

Sweeteners and Flavorings (optional):

1-2 teaspoons stevia or erythritol (sugar alternatives suitable for people with diabetes)

1/2 teaspoon vanilla extract

A pinch of cinnamon (optional for flavor)

Instructions:

1. **Combine Base Ingredients:** In a mixing bowl, combine the unsweetened almond milk, rolled oats, Greek yogurt, chia seeds (if using), almond butter or chopped almonds, sweetener (if using), and vanilla extract. Stir until all ingredients are well mixed.

2. **Incorporate Berries:** Gently fold the mixed berries into the oat mixture. If using frozen berries, there's no need to thaw them before adding them, as they will release their juices while chilling.

3. **Prepare Storage Containers:** Divide the oat mixture evenly between two airtight containers or mason jars.

4. **Chill:** Cover the containers with lids and refrigerate for at least 4 hours or overnight. This will allow the oats to absorb the liquid and soften.

5. **Serve:** In the morning, stir the oats gently and add almond milk if they are too thick. Top with additional berries or crushed nuts if desired.

Nutritional Information (per serving): Calories: 220, Protein: 12g, Carbohydrates: 30g, Fats: 8g, Fiber: 8g, Cholesterol: 0mg, Sodium: 200mg, Potassium: 320mg

Enjoy your healthy, delicious Berry Almond, Overnight Oats! This recipe is tailored to be nutritious while managing blood sugar levels effectively.

Spinach and Feta Egg Muffins

Prep time: 10 min	Cooking time: 20 min	Serves: 12

Ingredients

8 large eggs

1 cup fresh spinach, chopped

1/2 cup feta cheese, crumbled (reduced fat for lower calories)

1/4 cup diced onion (optional)

1/4 cup bell pepper, diced (optional)

1/4 cup milk (unsweetened almond milk or low-fat milk)

1/2 teaspoon garlic powder

1/2 teaspoon black pepper

1/4 teaspoon salt

1/4 teaspoon dried oregano (optional)

Cooking spray or olive oil (for greasing muffin tin)

Instructions:

1. **Preheat the Oven**: Preheat your oven to 350°F (175°C) and grease a muffin tin with cooking spray or olive oil to prevent sticking.

2. **Prepare the Egg Mixture**: In a large mixing bowl, crack the eggs and beat them until well mixed. Stir in the milk, garlic powder, pepper, salt, and oregano, blending until smooth.

3. **Add Vegetables and Cheese**: Fold in the chopped spinach, crumbled feta cheese, and any optional ingredients like diced onion or bell pepper. Mix until evenly distributed.

4. **Fill the Muffin Tin**: Pour the egg mixture into the greased muffin tin. Fill each cup about two-thirds full to allow for rising.

5. **Bake**: Place the muffin tin in the oven and bake for about 20 minutes until the muffins are set and lightly golden on top. You can check doneness by inserting a toothpick in the middle of a muffin—if it comes out clean, they are done.

6. **Cool and Serve**: Allow the muffins to cool in the tin briefly before transferring to a wire rack to cool completely. Serve warm or store in an airtight container in the refrigerator for up to a week.

Nutritional Information (per serving): Calories: 85, Protein: 8g, Carbohydrates: 3g, Fat: 5g, Fiber: 1g, Cholesterol: 195mg, Sodium: 150mg, Potassium: 210mg

Quinoa Breakfast Bowl with Nuts and Berries

Prep time: 5 min	Cooking time: 15 min	Serves: 2

Ingredients

1 cup cooked quinoa (approximately 1/3 cup dry quinoa, rinsed)

1/2 cup almond milk (unsweetened) or any other low-calorie milk alternative

1/2 cup mixed berries (blueberries, strawberries, or raspberries, fresh or frozen)

1/4 cup mixed nuts (almonds, walnuts, or pecans), chopped

one tablespoon of chia seeds (optional for extra fiber and omega-3 fatty acids)

one tablespoon of honey or **maple syrup** (optional, adjust to taste)

1/2 teaspoon cinnamon (optional for flavor)

one tablespoon flaxseed (optional for additional fiber)

Instructions:

1. **Cook the Quinoa**: Rinse 1/3 cup of dry quinoa under cold water to remove bitterness. In a small pot, combine the rinsed quinoa with 2/3 cup of water and a pinch of salt. Bring to a boil, reduce the heat to low, cover, and simmer for about 15 minutes or until the water is absorbed. Once cooked, fluff it with a fork and let it cool slightly.

2. **Prepare the Bowl**: Combine the cooked quinoa and almond milk in a medium bowl. Stir to mix until a creamy consistency is achieved. If you prefer a thicker consistency, you can reduce the amount of almond milk.

3. **Add Toppings**: Gently fold in the mixed berries and chia seeds. You can reserve some berries for garnishing.

4. **Sprinkle Nuts and Sweetener:** Top the quinoa mixture with the chopped mixed nuts and drizzle with honey or maple syrup if desired. Sprinkle with cinnamon and flaxseed if using.

5. **Serve:** Divide the mixture into two bowls. Optionally, garnish with additional berries and nuts on top for presentation.

Nutritional Information (per serving): Calories: 320, Protein: 10g, Carbohydrates: 34g, Fat: 15g, Fiber: 8g, Cholesterol: 0mg, Sodium: 75mg, Potassium: 350mg

Enjoy your nutritious and satisfying Quinoa Breakfast Bowl with Nuts and Berries!

Whole Wheat Banana Pancakes with Greek Yogurt

Prep time: 10 min	Cooking time: 15min	Serves: 4 (about 8 pancakes)

Ingredients

1 cup whole wheat flour
2 ripe bananas, mashed
2 large eggs
1/2 cup unsweetened almond milk (or low-fat milk)
1 teaspoon of baking powder
1/2 teaspoon baking soda
1/2 teaspoon cinnamon (optional for flavor)
Pinch of salt
1/2 cup unsweetened Greek yogurt (for topping)
1 teaspoon vanilla extract (optional)
Cooking spray or a small amount of oil (for the skillet)

Instructions:

1. **Prepare the Batter:** In a large bowl, mash the two ripe bananas with a fork until smooth. Add the eggs, almond milk, and vanilla extract (if using) to the mashed bananas and mix until well combined.

2. **Mix Dry Ingredients:** In a separate bowl, whisk together the whole wheat flour, baking powder, baking soda, cinnamon (if using), and salt.

3. **Combine Ingredients:** Gradually add the dry and wet ingredients, stirring gently until combined. Avoid over-mixing; small lumps are okay.

4. **Heat the Skillet:** Heat a skillet or non-stick pan over medium heat and lightly grease it with cooking spray or a small amount of oil.

5. **Cook the Pancakes**: Pour 1/4 cup of batter onto the skillet for each pancake. Cook until bubbles form on the surface (about 2-3 minutes), then flip and cook for 2-3 minutes or until golden brown and cooked through. Repeat with the remaining batter.
6. **Serve**: Stack the pancakes on a plate and top with Greek yogurt. Optionally, you can add fresh berries or a sprinkle of nuts for added flavor and nutrition.

Nutritional Information (per serving, 2 pancakes): Calories: 180, Protein: 9g, Carbohydrates: 30g, Fat: 3g, Fiber: 4g, Cholesterol: 70mg, Sodium: 150mg, Potassium: 320mg

Enjoy your healthy and delicious Whole Wheat Banana Pancakes with Greek Yogurt!

Avocado and Tomato Toast on Whole Grain Bread

Prep time: 5 min	Cooking time: 5 min	Serves: 2

Ingredients

4 slices whole grain bread (look for brands with no added sugars)

1 ripe avocado

1 medium tomato, sliced

1/2 teaspoon lemon juice (freshly squeezed)

Salt and pepper, to taste

1/4 teaspoon red pepper flakes (optional for a bit of heat)

Fresh herbs (like basil or cilantro, optional for garnish)

1 tablespoon balsamic vinegar (optional for added flavor)

Instructions:

1. **Toast the Bread** (optional): Toast 4 slices of whole grain bread in a toaster or on a skillet until golden brown and crispy. If you prefer fresh, you can skip this step.
2. **Prepare the Avocado**: While the bread is toasting, cut the avocado in half, remove the pit, and scoop the flesh into a bowl. Add lemon juice and mash the avocado with a fork until creamy but still chunky. Season with salt and pepper to taste.

3. **Assemble the Toast**: Spread a generous layer of the mashed avocado onto each slice of whole-grain bread.
4. **Top with Tomato**: Place slices of tomato on top of the avocado spread. Season the tomatoes with a pinch of salt and pepper.
5. **Add Optional Toppings**: If desired, sprinkle red pepper flakes on top for heat and drizzle with balsamic vinegar. Garnish with fresh herbs for added flavor and nutrients.
6. **Serve**: Serve immediately as a healthy breakfast or snack.

Nutritional Information (per serving, 2 slices): Calories: 330, Protein: 10g, Carbohydrates: 42g, Fat: 16g, Fiber: 12g, Cholesterol: 0mg, Sodium: 350mg, Potassium: 700mg

Enjoy your nutritious and delicious Avocado and Tomato Toast on Whole Grain Bread!

Chia Seed Pudding with Cinnamon and Berries

Prep time: 5 min	**Cooking time: 2 hours (or overnight)**	**Serves: 2**

Ingredients

1/4 cup chia seeds

1 cup unsweetened almond milk (or any low-fat milk alternative)

1/2 teaspoon cinnamon

1/2 teaspoon vanilla extract (optional for added flavor)

1-2 teaspoons sweetener (such as stevia or erythritol, optional, to taste)

1/2 cup mixed berries (fresh or frozen; choose low-glycemic options like blueberries, strawberries, or blackberries)

Pinch of salt (optional)

Instructions:

1. **Combine Ingredients**: In a mixing bowl or jar, combine the chia seeds, almond milk, cinnamon, vanilla extract (if using), sweetener (if using), and a pinch of salt. Stir well to combine all ingredients.
2. **Mix Thoroughly**: Whisk the mixture for about 1-2 minutes to ensure the chia seeds are evenly distributed and not clumped together.

3. **Refrigerate**: Cover the bowl or jar with a lid or plastic wrap and place it in the refrigerator. Let it sit for at least 2 hours or overnight for the best results, allowing the chia seeds to absorb the liquid and thicken into a pudding-like consistency.

4. **Prepare Toppings**: When ready to serve, if using frozen berries, you may want to let them thaw slightly. Fresh berries can be added directly.

5. **Serve**: Remix the chia seed pudding and portion it into bowls. Top with mixed berries.

Nutritional Information (per serving): Calories: 180, Protein: 6g, Carbohydrates: 14g, Fat: 9g, Fiber: 10g, Cholesterol: 0mg, Sodium: 50mg, Potassium: 240mg

Enjoy your refreshing and nutritious Chia Seed Pudding with Cinnamon and Berries!

Savory Oatmeal with Spinach and Poached Egg

Prep time: 5 min	Cooking time: 10 min	Serves: 2

Ingredients

1 cup rolled oats

2 cups water (or low-sodium vegetable broth for extra flavor)

2 cups of fresh spinach, chopped

2 large eggs

1/2 teaspoon garlic powder (optional)

1/2 teaspoon onion powder (optional)

Salt and pepper, to taste

1 tablespoon olive oil (optional for drizzling)

Sliced avocado (optional for topping)

Fresh herbs (like parsley or chives, optional for garnish)

Instructions:

1. **Cook the Oats**: Combine the rolled oats and water (or vegetable broth) in a medium saucepan. Bring to a boil, then reduce the heat to low and simmer for about 5 minutes, stirring occasionally, until the oats are creamy and cooked to your liking.

2. **Add Spinach**: Stir in the chopped spinach during the last minute of cooking. If using garlic and onion powder, add them at this stage, along with salt and pepper to taste. Mix well until the spinach is wilted and everything is combined.

3. **Prepare the Poached Eggs**: Fill a separate saucepan with water while cooking oats and gently simmer. Crack each egg into a small bowl and gently slide it into the

simmering water. Poach the eggs for about 3-4 minutes, or until the whites are set and the yolks remain runny (cooking time may vary based on preference). Use a slotted spoon to remove each egg and let it drain.

4. **Assemble the Bowls**: Divide the savory oatmeal into two bowls. Top each bowl with a poached egg. Drizzle with olive oil, if desired, and sprinkle with additional salt, pepper, and fresh herbs for garnish.
5. **Serve**: Serve immediately, optionally adding sliced avocado for extra healthy fats.

Nutritional Information (per serving): Calories: 290, Protein: 14g, Carbohydrates: 36g, Fat: 10g, Fiber: 8g, Cholesterol: 186mg, Sodium: 120mg, Potassium: 550mg

Enjoy your hearty and nutritious Savory Oatmeal with Spinach and Poached Egg!

Greek Yogurt Parfait with Low-Sugar Granola

Prep time: 10 min	Cooking time: 10 min	Serves: 2

Ingredients
2 cups plain Greek yogurt (non-fat or low-fat)
1/2 cup low-sugar granola (store-bought or homemade)
1 cup mixed berries (such as blueberries, strawberries, or raspberries)
1 tablespoon chia seeds (optional for extra fiber and omega-3 fatty acids)
1 teaspoon honey or other low-calorie sweetener (optional, adjust to taste)
1/2 teaspoon vanilla extract (optional for flavor)

Instructions:
1. **Prepare the Yogurt**: In a mixing bowl, combine the Greek yogurt with vanilla extract and honey (if using). Stir until well mixed.
2. **Layer the Parfait**: In two serving cups or bowls, start with a layer of Greek yogurt at the bottom (about 1/2 cup each). Add a layer of mixed berries over the yogurt (about 1/2 cup each). Sprinkle a layer of low-sugar granola (about 1/4 cup each) over the berries. You can sprinkle chia seeds over the granola if you use chia seeds.

3. **Repeat Layers**: Layering with the remaining yogurt, berries, and granola until the cups are filled. You can make 2-3 layers, depending on the size of your serving cups.
4. **Serve**: Serve immediately as a healthy breakfast or snack.

Nutritional Information (per serving): Calories: 300, Protein: 20g, Carbohydrates: 40g, Fat: 7g, Fiber: 6g, Cholesterol: 10mg, Sodium: 70mg, Potassium: 450mg

Enjoy your delicious and nutritious Greek Yogurt Parfait with Low-Sugar Granola.

Egg and Vegetable Scramble with Salsa

Prep time: 5 min	Cooking time: 10 min	Serves: 2

Ingredients
4 large eggs
1/4 cup milk (unsweetened almond milk or low-fat milk)
1/2 cup bell pepper, diced (any color)
1/2 cup spinach, chopped (fresh or frozen)
Diced 1/4 cup of onion
1/4 cup tomatoes, diced (or canned diced tomatoes, drained)
Salt and pepper, to taste
1 teaspoon olive oil (for cooking)

1/4 cup salsa (store-bought or homemade, freshly made is best)
Fresh herbs (like cilantro or parsley, optional for garnish)

Instructions:

1. **Prepare the Ingredients**: Dice the bell pepper, onion, and tomatoes. Chop the spinach if you have fresh spinach.
2. **Whisk the Eggs**: Whisk together the eggs and milk until well combined, season with a pinch of salt and pepper.
3. **Cook the Vegetables**: Heat the olive oil over medium heat in a non-stick skillet. Add the diced onion and bell pepper, and sauté for about 2-3 minutes, or until the vegetables are softened. Add the chopped spinach and diced tomatoes to the skillet; cook for 1-2 minutes until the spinach wilts.
4. **Add Eggs**: Pour the egg mixture into the skillet over the vegetables. Allow it to sit until it begins to set around the edges, then gently stir with a spatula to scramble the eggs until fully cooked, about 3-5 minutes.
5. **Serve with Salsa**: Once the eggs are cooked through, remove from heat. Serve the scramble in bowls, topped with fresh salsa and, if desired, a sprinkle of fresh herbs.

Nutritional Information (per serving): Calories: 290, Protein: 18g, Carbohydrates: 10g, Fat: 20g, Fiber: 2g, Cholesterol: 370mg, Sodium: 350mg, Potassium: 550mg

Enjoy your healthy and satisfying Egg and Vegetable Scramble with Salsa!

Mini Vegetable Frittatas with Swiss Cheese

Prep time: 10 min   **Cooking time: 20 min**   **Serves: 12**

Ingredients
6 large eggs
1/4 cup unsweetened almond milk (or low-fat milk)
1/2 cup Swiss cheese, shredded (reduced fat if preferred)
1 cup mixed vegetables, chopped (such as bell peppers, spinach, and zucchini)
1/4 cup of onion, finely chopped
1/2 teaspoon garlic powder (optional)
Salt and pepper, to taste
1 tablespoon olive oil (for sautéing vegetables)
Fresh herbs (such as parsley or thyme, optional for garnish)

Instructions:

1. **Preheat the Oven**: Preheat your oven to 350°F (175°C) and grease a muffin tin with cooking spray or a small amount of olive oil.

2. **Sauté the Vegetables**: Heat 1 tablespoon of olive oil over medium heat in a skillet. Add the chopped onion and mixed vegetables. Sauté for about 5-7 minutes or until the vegetables are tender. If using garlic powder, add it during the last minute of cooking. Remove from heat.

3. **Prepare the Egg Mixture**: In a large mixing bowl, whisk together the eggs, almond milk, salt, and pepper.

4. **Combine Ingredients**: Stir the sautéed vegetables into the egg mixture. Add the shredded Swiss cheese and mix until well combined.

5. **Fill the Muffin Tin**: Pour the egg and vegetable mixture evenly into the prepared muffin tin, filling each cup about 3/4 full.

6. **Bake**: In the oven for 15-20 minutes or until the frittatas are set and the tops are lightly golden. A toothpick inserted in the center should come out clean.

7. **Cool and Serve**: Allow the mini frittatas to cool for a few minutes before removing them from the muffin tin. Serve warm or at room temperature. Garnish with fresh herbs if desired.

Nutritional Information (per mini frittata): Calories: 90, Protein: 7g, Carbohydrates: 3g, Fat: 6g, Fiber: 1g, Cholesterol: 150mg, Sodium: 120mg, Potassium: 180mg

Enjoy your healthy and delicious Mini Vegetable Frittatas with Swiss Cheese!

Zucchini and Corn Fritters with Greek Yogurt Sauce

Prep time: 10 min	Cooking time: 15 min	Serves: 4 (about 8 fritters)

Ingredients
For the Fritters:
2 medium zucchinis, grated (about 2 cups)
1 cup of corn kernels (fresh, frozen, or canned, drained)
1/4 cup green onions, finely chopped
1/4 cup of whole wheat flour (or almond flour for a gluten-free option)
1 large egg

1/2 teaspoon garlic powder (optional)

1/2 teaspoon onion powder (optional)
1/2 teaspoon cumin (optional for flavor)
Salt and pepper, to taste
1 tablespoon olive oil (for cooking)
For the Greek Yogurt Sauce:
1 cup plain Greek yogurt (non-fat or low-fat)
1 tablespoon lemon juice
1 tablespoon fresh dill, chopped (or 1 teaspoon dried dill)
Salt and pepper, to taste

Instructions:

1. **Prepare the Zucchini:** Grate it and place it in a clean dish towel. Squeeze out the excess moisture to ensure the fritters are not soggy.
2. **Mix Fritter Ingredients:** In a large mixing bowl, combine the grated zucchini, corn, green onions, whole wheat flour, egg, garlic powder, onion powder, cumin, salt, and pepper. Mix until well combined.
3. **Heat the Oil:** Heat the olive oil over medium heat in a large skillet.
4. **Cook the Fritters:** Scoop about 1/4 cup of the fritter mixture and place it in the skillet. Flatten slightly with a spatula. Repeat until the skillet is filled, but be careful not to overcrowd. Cook for 3-4 minutes on each side until golden brown is cooked. Repeat with the remaining batter, adding more oil to the skillet as needed.
5. **Prepare the Greek Yogurt Sauce:** In a small bowl, mix the Greek yogurt, lemon juice, dill, salt, and pepper until smooth.
6. Serve the fritters warm with a dollop of Greek yogurt sauce on top or on the side.

Nutritional Information (per serving, 2 fritters): Calories: 180, Protein: 10g, Carbohydrates: 20g, Fat: 6g, Fiber: 4g, Cholesterol: 60mg, Sodium: 210mg, Potassium: 370mg

Enjoy your nutritious and tasty Zucchini and Corn Fritters with Greek Yogurt Sauce!

Breakfast Burrito with Eggs, Beans, and Salsa

Prep time: 10 min	Cooking time: 10 min	Serves: 2

Ingredients

4 large eggs

1/2 cup black beans (canned, drained, and rinsed)

1/2 cup salsa (fresh or store-bought, mild or spicy)

2 whole wheat tortillas (preferably low-carb)

1/4 cup bell pepper, diced (any color)

Diced 1/4 cup of onion

1 tablespoon olive oil (for cooking)

Salt and pepper, to taste

1/4 teaspoon cumin (optional for flavor)

1/4 cup avocado, sliced (optional for serving)

Fresh cilantro (optional for garnish)

Instructions:

1. **Prepare Ingredients**: Dice the bell pepper and onion. Drain and rinse the black beans if canned beans are used.

2. **Sauté Vegetables**: Heat olive oil in a non-stick skillet over medium heat. Add the diced onion and bell pepper, and sauté for 3-4 minutes until softening.

3. **Whisk Eggs**: In a bowl, whisk together the eggs, salt, pepper, and cumin (if using) until well combined.

4. **Add Beans and Eggs**: Add the rinsed black beans to the skillet with the sautéed vegetables, stirring gently until heated through. Pour the egg mixture over the beans and vegetables. Cook, stirring gently, until the eggs are set, for about 3-4 minutes.

5. **Warm Tortillas**: While cooking the egg mixture, warm the whole wheat tortillas in a separate skillet or microwave until pliable.

6. **Assemble Burritos**: Evenly divide the eggs, black beans, and vegetable mixture between the tortillas. Top each with salsa and, if desired, slices of avocado. Roll the tortillas tightly to create burritos.

7. **Serve**: Cut the burritos in half and serve warm, garnished with fresh cilantro if desired.

Nutritional Information (per serving, 1 burrito): Calories: 360, Protein: 20g, Carbohydrates: 38g, Fat: 16g, Fiber: 10g, Cholesterol: 370mg, Sodium: 530mg, Potassium: 570mg.

Enjoy your healthy and satisfying Breakfast Burrito with Eggs, Beans, and Salsa!

Oven-Baked Egg and Veggie Cup

Prep time: 10 min   **Cooking time: 20 min**   **Serves: 12 eggs cups**

Ingredients

8 large eggs

1/4 cup unsweetened almond milk (or low-fat milk)

1 cup fresh spinach, chopped

1/2 cup bell pepper, diced (any color)

1/2 cup cherry tomatoes, halved (or regular diced tomatoes)

Diced 1/4 cup of onion

1/2 teaspoon garlic powder (optional)

Salt and pepper, to taste

1/2 cup shredded reduced-fat cheese (optional)

Cooking spray or olive oil (for greasing the muffin tin)

Instructions:

1. **Preheat the Oven**: Preheat your oven to 350°F (175°C). Grease a standard 12-cup muffin tin with cooking spray or a small amount of olive oil.
2. **Prepare the Vegetables**: Chop the spinach, bell pepper, onion, and cherry tomatoes.
3. **Whisk the Eggs**: Whisk together the eggs and almond milk until well combined in a large bowl—season with salt, pepper, and garlic powder (if using).
4. **Combine Ingredients**: Add the chopped spinach, bell pepper, onion, and tomatoes to the egg mixture. If you use cheese, fold it in at this stage.
5. **Fill the Muffin Tin**: Evenly distribute the egg and veggie mixture into the prepared muffin cups, filling each about 3/4 full.
6. **Bake**: Place the muffin tin in the oven and bake for 20-25 minutes until the egg cups are set and lightly golden on top. You can test doneness by inserting a toothpick in the center of one of the cups; it should come out clean.

7. **Cool and Serve**: Allow the egg cups to cool in the tin for a few minutes before removing them. Use a small knife to loosen the edges, if necessary, gently.
8. **Enjoy**: Serve warm or store in an airtight container for meal prep.

Nutritional Information (per egg cup): Calories: 90, Protein: 7g, Carbohydrates: 4g, Fat: 6g, Fiber: 1g, Cholesterol: 186mg, Sodium: 150mg, Potassium: 170mg

Enjoy your nutritious and delicious Oven-Baked Egg and Veggie Cups!

Almond Flour Muffins with Blueberries

Prep time: 10 min	Cooking time: 20 min	Serves: 12 muffins

Ingredients

2 cups of almond flour
1/2 teaspoon baking soda
1/2 teaspoon of baking powder
1/4 teaspoon salt
3 large eggs
1/4 cup unsweetened almond milk (or low-fat milk)
1/4 cup erythritol or another low-calorie sweetener (adjust to taste)
1 teaspoon vanilla extract
1 cup fresh or frozen blueberries (if using frozen, do not thaw)
1 tablespoon lemon zest (optional for flavor)
1/4 cup chopped nuts (optional for added texture and nutrition)

Instructions:

1. **Preheat the Oven**: Preheat your oven to 350°F (175°C). Line a 12-cup muffin tin with paper liners or grease with cooking spray.
2. **Mix Dry Ingredients**: In a large mixing bowl, combine the almond flour, baking soda, baking powder, and salt. Stir until well combined.
3. **Whisk Wet Ingredients**:
   o In another bowl, whisk together the eggs, almond milk, erythritol (or sweetener), vanilla extract, and lemon zest (if using) until smooth.
4. **Combine Mixtures**: Pour the wet ingredients into the dry ingredients. Stir gently until it is just combined; do not over-mix.
5. **Fold in Blueberries**: Gently fold in the blueberries and nuts if using, being careful not to break the berries.

6. **Fill Muffin Tin**: Evenly distribute the batter into the prepared muffin tin, filling each cup about 3/4 full.
7. **Bake**: Bake in the oven for 18-20 minutes or until the muffins are golden brown and a toothpick inserted into the center comes clean.
8. **Cool and Serve**: Allow the muffins to cool in the tin for 5 minutes before transferring them to a wire rack to cool completely.

Nutritional Information (per muffin): Calories: 140, Protein: 6g, Carbohydrates: 6g, Fat: 12g, Fiber: 3g, Cholesterol: 55mg, Sodium: 150mg, Potassium: 180mg

Enjoy your healthy and delicious Almond Flour Muffins with Blueberries!

Herbed Avocado Omelette with Feta Cheese

Prep time: 5 min	Cooking time: 10 min	Serves: 2

Ingredients

4 large eggs
1/4 cup unsweetened almond milk (or low-fat milk)
1 small avocado, diced
1/2 cup feta cheese, crumbled
• **1/4 cup fresh herbs**, chopped (such as parsley, dill, or chives)
Salt and pepper, to taste
1 tablespoon olive oil (or cooking spray)
1/4 cup diced tomatoes (optional for garnish)
1 tablespoon fresh lemon juice (optional for added flavor)

Instructions:

1. **Prepare Ingredients**: Dice the avocado and tomatoes and chop the fresh herbs.
2. **Whisk Eggs**: In a mixing bowl, whisk the eggs, almond milk, salt, and pepper until well combined.
3. **Heat the Pan**: In a non-stick skillet, heat olive oil or spray with cooking spray over medium heat.
4. **Cook the Omelette**: Pour the egg mixture into the heated skillet, tilting the pan to spread evenly. Cook for about 2-3 minutes or until the edges begin to set.

5. **Add Filling**: Sprinkle half of the crumbled feta cheese and half of the diced avocado over one-half of the Omelette. Add the fresh herbs on top of the fillings.
6. **Fold and Finish Cooking**: Carefully fold the Omelette in half over the filling. Continue cooking for 2-3 minutes until the eggs are cooked and the cheese melts.
7. **Serve**: Transfer the Omelette to a plate. Repeat with the remaining ingredients to make a second Omelette. Optionally, garnish with diced tomatoes and a drizzle of lemon juice.

Nutritional Information (per serving): Calories: 320, Protein: 20g, Carbohydrates: 10g, Fat: 25g, Fiber: 5g, Cholesterol: 330mg, Sodium: 500mg, Potassium: 650mg

Enjoy your delicious and nutritious Herbed Avocado Omelette with Feta Cheese!

Lunch: Balanced meals to keep you full until dinner.

Grilled Chicken Quinoa Bowl

Prep time: 15 min   **Cooking time: 25 min**   **Serves: 4**

Ingredients
For the Bowl:
1 cup of quinoa (rinsed)
2 cups of water or low-sodium chicken broth
1 lb. boneless, skinless chicken breasts
2 tablespoons of olive oil
1 teaspoon garlic powder
1 teaspoon paprika
½ teaspoon black pepper
½ teaspoon salt (optional, adjust to taste)
1 cup cherry tomatoes, halved
1 cup cucumbers, diced
1 cup spinach or mixed greens
¼ cup red onion, thinly sliced (optional)

Instructions:

1. **Cook the Quinoa:** In a medium saucepan, combine the rinsed quinoa and water or chicken broth. Bring to boil over medium-high heat. Once boiling, reduce heat to low, cover, and simmer for about 15 minutes or until liquid is absorbed and quinoa is fluffy. Remove from heat and let sit covered for 5 minutes—fluff with a fork.

2. **Prepare the Chicken:** Preheat the grill or grill pan over medium-high heat while the quinoa is cooking. Mix olive oil, garlic powder, paprika, black pepper, and salt in a small bowl to create a marinade. Coat the chicken breasts with the marinade evenly on both sides.

3. **Grill the Chicken:** Place the marinated chicken on the grill. Grill for 6-7 minutes per side or until the internal temperature reaches 165°F (75°C). After grilling, let the chicken rest for a few minutes, then slice it into strips.

4. **Assemble the Bowls:** Start with a quinoa base in each serving bowl. Add sliced grilled chicken on top. Top with cherry tomatoes, cucumbers, spinach, and red onion (if using). Optionally, add sliced avocado and drizzle with lemon juice or balsamic vinegar.

5. **Serve:** Serve the bowls warm and enjoy!

Nutritional Information (per serving) Calories: 400, **Protein:** 32 g, **Carbohydrates:** 35 g, **Fats:** 15 g, **Fiber:** 6 g, **Cholesterol:** 70 mg, **Sodium:** 200 mg (without added salt), **Potassium:** 800 mg

Enjoy your healthy and delicious Grilled Chicken Quinoa Bowl!

Beef Stir-Fry with Broccoli

Prep time: 20 min   **Cooking time: 15 min**   **Serves: 4**

Ingredients
Main Ingredients:
1 lb. lean beef sirloin, thinly sliced across the grain
3 cups of broccoli florets
1 red bell pepper, sliced
1 small onion, thinly sliced
2 tablespoons of olive oil
Marinade:
2 tablespoons low-sodium soy sauce
1 tablespoon sesame oil
1 tablespoon rice vinegar
1 tablespoon ginger, minced
2 garlic cloves, minced
1 teaspoon cornstarch

- **Optional Ingredients:**
    1 tablespoon sesame seeds
    1 tablespoon green onions, sliced
    1 teaspoon red pepper flakes (for spice)

Instructions:

1. **Prepare the Marinade:** In a bowl, combine soy sauce, sesame oil, rice vinegar, ginger, garlic, and cornstarch. Mix well. Add sliced beef to the marinade, coat evenly, and let it sit for at least 15 minutes.

2. **Cook the Beef:** Heat 1 tablespoon of olive oil in a large skillet or wok over medium-high heat. Add the marinated beef to the skillet and stir-fry for 2-3 minutes until browned. Remove beef from the skillet and set it aside.

3. **Stir-Fry Vegetables:** Add the remaining tablespoon of olive oil in the same skillet. Add broccoli, bell pepper, and onion. Stir-fry for 5-7 minutes until the vegetables are tender-crisp.

4. **Combine Ingredients:** Return the beef to the skillet with the vegetables. Stir and cook for another 2 minutes, ensuring everything is well mixed and heated.

5. **Finalize and Serve:** Add sesame seeds and green onions for garnish if desired. Serve hot and enjoy!

Nutritional Information (per serving): Calories: 350, **Protein:** 30 g, **Carbohydrates:** 18 g, **Fats:** 18 g, **Fiber:** 5 g, **Cholesterol:** 70 mg, **Sodium:** 450 mg, **Potassium:** 850 mg

Enjoy this quick and flavorful meal that supports a healthy, diabetic-friendly diet!

Turkey and Spinach Stuffed Peppers

Prep time: 20 min   **Cooking time: 30 min**   **Serves: 4**

Ingredients

Main Ingredients:

4 medium bell peppers, halved and seeded

1 lb. ground turkey (preferably lean)

2 cups of fresh spinach, chopped

1 small onion, diced

2 cloves garlic, minced

1 can (14.5 oz) diced tomatoes, drained

1 cup cooked quinoa (or brown rice as an alternative)

1 tablespoon olive oil

1 teaspoon dried oregano

1 teaspoon paprika

½ teaspoon black pepper

½ teaspoon salt (optional, adjust to taste)

Optional Ingredients:

¼ cup feta cheese, crumbled

1 tablespoon fresh parsley, chopped

Instructions:

1. **Prepare the Peppers:** Preheat your oven to 375°F (190°C). Place the halved and seeded bell peppers in a baking dish, cut side up.
2. **Cook Turkey. Filling:** In a large skillet, heat olive oil over medium heat. Add onion and garlic, sautéing until soft, about 3 minutes. Add ground turkey to the skillet, cooking until browned and fully cooked, breaking it up with a spoon.
3. **Mix in Remaining Ingredients:** Stir the chopped spinach, drained diced tomatoes, cooked quinoa, oregano, paprika, black pepper, and salt into the turkey mixture. Cook for another 5 minutes, allowing flavors to meld.
4. **Stuff the Peppers:** Spoon the turkey and spinach mixture into each bell pepper half, packing them generously.
5. **Bake the Peppers:** Cover the baking dish with foil and bake for 20 minutes. Uncover and bake for 10 minutes, until the peppers are tender.

6. **Garnish and Serve:** If desired, sprinkle stuffed peppers with feta cheese and fresh parsley before serving.

Nutritional Information (per serving): Calories: 320 Protein: 28 g, Carbohydrates: 28 g, Fats: 10 g, Fiber: 7 g, Cholesterol: 60 mg, Sodium: 400 mg, Potassium: 900 mg

Enjoy your Turkey and Spinach Stuffed Peppers!

Lentil Salad with Feta and Chicken

Prep time: 15 min	Cooking time: 30 min	Serves: 4

Ingredients

Main Ingredients:

1 cup of dry lentils, rinsed

2 cups cooked chicken breast, diced

1 cup cherry tomatoes, halved

1 small cucumber, diced

1 small red onion, finely chopped

1 cup fresh spinach, chopped

¼ cup feta cheese, crumbled

2 tablespoons fresh parsley, chopped

Dressing:

3 tablespoons of olive oil

2 tablespoons lemon juice

1 teaspoon Dijon mustard

1 teaspoon dried oregano

½ teaspoon black pepper

½ teaspoon salt (optional)

Optional Ingredients:

¼ cup Kalamata olives, pitted and sliced

1 tablespoon capers

Instructions:

1. **Cook the Lentils:** Combine lentils and 3 cups of water in a medium saucepan. Bring to a boil, reduce heat, and simmer for 20-25 minutes or until lentils are tender. Drain and let cool.

2. **Prepare the Dressing:** In a small bowl, whisk together olive oil, lemon juice, Dijon mustard, oregano, black pepper, and salt to make the dressing.

3. **Assemble the Salad:** In a large bowl, combine cooked lentils, diced chicken, cherry tomatoes, cucumber, red onion, spinach, and parsley. Drizzle the dressing over the salad and toss gently to combine.

4. **Add Feta and Optional Ingredients:** Sprinkle feta cheese over the salad. If using, add olives and capers for extra flavor.

5. **Serve:** Serve the salad chilled or at room temperature. Enjoy!

Nutritional Information (per serving): Calories: 380, **Protein:** 35 g, **Carbohydrates:** 30 g, **Fats:** 15 g, **Fiber:** 10 g, **Cholesterol:** 70 mg, **Sodium:** 450 mg, **Potassium:** 850 mg

Tuna and White Bean Salad

Prep time: 15 min   **Cooking time: 0 min**   **Serves: 4**

Ingredients
Main Ingredients:
2 cans (5 oz each) of tuna packed in water, drained
1 can (15 oz) white beans (cannellini or navy), rinsed and drained
1 small red onion, finely chopped
1 cup cherry tomatoes, halved
1 cucumber, diced
2 cups mixed salad greens (spinach, arugula, or your choice)
Dressing:
3 tablespoons of olive oil
2 tablespoons red wine vinegar
1 teaspoon Dijon mustard
1 teaspoon dried oregano

½ teaspoon black pepper
½ teaspoon salt (optional)
Optional Ingredients:
¼ cup fresh parsley, chopped
1 tablespoon capers, rinsed
¼ teaspoon red pepper flakes (for spice)

Instructions:

1. **Combine Salad Ingredients:** In a large bowl, add drained tuna, rinsed and drained white beans, chopped red onion, halved cherry tomatoes, diced cucumber, and mixed salad greens.

2. **Prepare the Dressing:** In a small bowl, whisk together olive oil, red wine vinegar, Dijon mustard, oregano, black pepper, and salt until well combined.

3. **Mix the Salad:** Pour the dressing over the salad mixture and gently toss until all ingredients are evenly coated.

4. **Add Optional Ingredients:** If desired, add chopped parsley, capers, and red pepper flakes for additional flavor and complexity.

5. **Serve:** Divide salad into 4 servings and enjoy immediately or refrigerate for a chilled option.

Nutritional Information (per serving): Calories: 320, **Protein:** 30 g, **Carbohydrates:** 20 g, **Fats:** 15 g, **Fiber:** 8 g, **Cholesterol:** 50 mg, **Sodium:** 400 mg, **Potassium:** 650 mg

Serving Suggestions
- Serve with whole-grain crackers or a slice of whole-grain bread for added texture.
- Pair with a cup of vegetable soup for a balanced meal.

Diabetic-Friendly Notes

This salad is rich in protein from tuna and fiber from white beans, which help manage blood sugar levels. Fresh vegetables add essential vitamins and minerals without excessive calories. The dressing is simple and heart-healthy, utilizing olive oil and vinegar that do not spike blood sugar. This dish is nutritious, easy to prepare, and perfect for a diabetic-friendly diet. Enjoy your healthy Tuna and White Bean Salad!

Chickpea and Chicken Curry

Prep time: 15 min   **Cooking time: 30 min**   **Serves: 4**

Ingredients

Main Ingredients:

1 lb. boneless, skinless chicken breast, diced

1 can (15 oz) chickpeas, rinsed and drained

1 cup diced tomatoes (canned or fresh)

1 medium onion, finely chopped

2 cloves garlic, minced

1 tablespoon ginger, minced

1 teaspoon olive oil

1 tablespoon curry powder

1 teaspoon cumin

½ teaspoon turmeric (optional)

½ teaspoon black pepper

½ teaspoon salt (optional)

1 cup low-sodium chicken broth (or water)

1 cup spinach (fresh or frozen)

Optional Ingredients:

½ cup coconut milk (for creaminess)

Fresh cilantro for garnish

Red pepper flakes (for spice)

Instructions:

1. **Prepare the Ingredients:** Dice chicken breast and chop the onion, garlic, and ginger.

2. **Sauté Aromatics:** Heat olive oil over medium heat in a large skillet. Add the chopped onion, garlic, and ginger. Sauté for about 3-5 minutes until the onion is translucent.
3. **Cook the Chicken:** Add the diced chicken to the skillet. Cook until the chicken is browned on the outside, for about 5-7 minutes.
4. **Add Spices:** Stir in the curry powder, cumin, turmeric, black pepper, and salt. Cook for another 1-2 minutes to toast the spices.
5. **Add Chickpeas and Tomatoes:** Add the chickpeas and diced tomatoes to the skillet. Pour in the chicken broth. If using, add the coconut milk for creaminess. Stir to combine.
6. **Simmer:** Bring the mixture to a simmer, cover, and cook for 15-20 minutes, allowing the flavors to meld and the chicken to cook through.
7. **Add Spinach:** Stir in the spinach and cook for 5 minutes, until wilted.
8. **Serve** the curry warm, garnished with fresh cilantro and red pepper flakes if desired.

Nutritional Information (per serving): Calories: 350, Protein: 30 g, Carbohydrates: 35 g, Fats: 10 g, Fiber: 10 g, Cholesterol: 75 mg, Sodium: 400 mg, Potassium: 850 mg

Enjoy your delicious and healthy curry!

Shrimp and Avocado Salad

Prep time: 15 min	Cooking time: 5 min	Serves: 4

Ingredients

Main Ingredients:

1 lb. shrimp, peeled and deveined
2 ripe avocados, diced
1 cup cherry tomatoes, halved
1 small cucumber, diced
¼ cup red onion, finely chopped
2 cups of mixed greens (spinach, arugula, or your choice)

Dressing:

3 tablespoons of olive oil
2 tablespoons fresh lime juice
1 teaspoon Dijon mustard
½ teaspoon garlic powder
½ teaspoon black pepper
½ teaspoon salt (optional)

Optional Ingredients:

¼ cup fresh cilantro, chopped
1 small jalapeño, diced (for heat)
¼ cup feta cheese, crumbled (for flavor)

Instructions:

1. **Cook the Shrimp:** Heat 1 tablespoon of olive oil over medium-high heat in a non-stick skillet. Add the shrimp and season with salt and pepper. Cook for 2-3 minutes on each side or until the shrimp are pink and cooked. Remove from heat and let cool slightly.

2. **Prepare the Dressing:** In a small bowl, whisk the remaining olive oil, lime juice, Dijon mustard, garlic powder, black pepper, and salt until well combined.

3. **Assemble the Salad:** In a large mixing bowl, combine the cooked shrimp, diced avocados, halved cherry tomatoes, diced cucumber, chopped red onion, and mixed greens.

4. **Drizzle with Dressing:** Pour the dressing over the salad and gently toss until everything is coated evenly.

5. **Add Optional Ingredients:** If using, sprinkle fresh cilantro, diced jalapeño, and crumbled feta cheese over the top.

6. **Serve:** Divide the salad into bowls or plates and serve immediately.

Nutritional Information (per serving): Calories: 320, Protein: 24 g, Carbohydrates: 18 g, Fats: 20 g, Fiber: 9 g, Cholesterol: 160 mg, Sodium: 350 mg, Potassium: 750 mg

Enjoy this fresh and nutritious salad!

Diabetic-Friendly Minestrone Soup

Prep time: 15 min   **Cooking time: 30 min**   **Serves: 6**

Ingredients:

1 tablespoon olive oil
1 medium onion, diced
2 cloves garlic, minced
2 medium carrots, diced
2 celery stalks, diced
1 medium zucchini, diced
1 cup green beans, chopped
1 can (14.5 oz) diced tomatoes (no added sugar)
4 cups low-sodium vegetable broth
1 teaspoon dried oregano
1 teaspoon dried basil
1/2 teaspoon salt (adjust to taste)
1/4 teaspoon black pepper
1 can (15 oz) cannellini beans, rinsed and drained
1 cup chopped spinach or kale (fresh or frozen)

Optional: 1/2 cup small whole-grain pasta (like whole wheat or low-carb pasta)

Instructions:

1. **Sauté the Vegetables:** Heat the olive oil over medium heat in a large pot. Add the diced onion and garlic, and sauté for about 2-3 minutes until the onion is translucent.

2. **Add the Remaining Vegetables:** Add the carrots, celery, zucchini, and green beans to the pot. Cook for an additional 5 minutes, stirring occasionally.

3. **Combine Ingredients:** Stir in the diced tomatoes (with their juices), vegetable broth, oregano, basil, salt, and black pepper. Bring the soup to a simmer.

4. **Simmer the Soup:** Cover the pot and let it simmer for about 15 minutes, allowing the vegetables to soften and the flavors to meld.

5. **Add the Beans and Greens:** After 15 minutes, add the rinsed cannellini beans and chopped spinach or kale to the soup. If using pasta, you can also add it at this stage. Simmer for 5-10 minutes until the pasta is cooked (if included) and the greens are wilted.

6. **Adjust Seasoning:** Taste the soup and adjust the seasoning as necessary. You may add more salt or pepper, depending on your preference.

7. **Serve:** Ladle the soup into bowls and serve hot. You can garnish with fresh herbs or a sprinkle of parmesan cheese if desired (remember the carbs and calories if adding cheese).

Nutritional Information (per serving): Calories: 130, **Protein:** 8g, **Carbohydrates:** 22g, **Fats:** 3g, **Fiber:** 6g, **Cholesterol:** 0mg, **Sodium:** 240mg, **Potassium:** 450mg.

Enjoy your healthy Minestrone!

Zucchini Noodles with Turkey Bolognese

Prep time: 15 min	Cooking time: 25 min	Serves: 4

Ingredients

Main Ingredients:

4 medium zucchinis, spiralized into noodles
1 lb. ground turkey (lean)
1 can (14.5 oz) diced tomatoes
1 small onion, finely chopped
2 cloves garlic, minced
1 carrot, finely diced
1 celery stalk, finely diced
2 tablespoons of olive oil
1 teaspoon dried oregano
1 teaspoon dried basil
½ teaspoon black pepper
½ teaspoon salt (optional)
¼ teaspoon red pepper flakes (optional, for heat)

Optional Ingredients: Grated Parmesan cheese (for serving), Fresh basil leaves (for garnish)

Instructions:

1. **Prepare the Zucchini Noodles:** Spiralize them into noodles and set them aside. You can also use a vegetable peeler to create ribbon-like noodles if preferred.

2. **Cook the Turkey Bolognese:** Heat the olive oil over medium heat in a large skillet. Add chopped onion, garlic, carrot, and celery. Sauté for about 5-7 minutes until vegetables are softened. Add the ground turkey to the skillet. Cook until browned, breaking it up with a spoon, for about 5-7 minutes.

3. **Add Tomatoes and Seasonings:** Stir in the canned diced tomatoes (with juice), oregano, basil, black pepper, and salt. If using, add red pepper flakes for heat. Bring to a simmer and cook for about 10 minutes, allowing flavors to melt and sauce to thicken.

4. **Cook the Zucchini Noodles:** In a separate skillet, lightly sauté the zucchini noodles in olive oil or steam them for 2-3 minutes until tender. You want them to retain some crunch to mimic traditional pasta.

5. **Combine and Serve:** Divide the zucchini noodles among serving plates. Spoon the turkey Bolognese sauce over the noodles. Top with grated Parmesan cheese and garnish with fresh basil if desired.

Nutritional Information (per serving): Calories: 290, Protein: 28 g, Carbohydrates: 12 g, Fats: 16 g, Fiber: 3 g, Cholesterol: 85 mg, Sodium: 400 mg, Potassium: 800 mg

Serving Suggestions

- Serve with a side salad of mixed greens topped with a vinaigrette for extra fiber and nutrients.

- Pair with a few olives or a slice of whole-grain bread (if desired) for added texture.

Enjoy your healthy and delicious Zucchini Noodles with Turkey Bolognese!

Pork Tenderloin with Roasted Vegetables

Prep time: 15 min	Cooking time: 30 min	Serves: 4

Ingredients

Main Ingredients:

1 lb. pork tenderloin
2 cups of mixed vegetables (such as carrots, zucchini, bell peppers, and broccoli)
2 tablespoons of olive oil
2 cloves garlic, minced
1 teaspoon dried rosemary (or thyme)
1 teaspoon paprika
½ teaspoon black pepper
½ teaspoon salt (optional)
Juice of 1 lemon (for flavor)
Optional Ingredients: Fresh parsley, chopped (for garnish), additional herbs (like oregano or basil) for seasoning, red pepper flakes (for extra heat)

Instructions:

1. **Preheat the Oven:** Preheat your oven to 400°F (200°C).

2. **Prepare the Pork Tenderloin:** Pat the pork tenderloin dry with paper towels. Season it with garlic, rosemary, paprika, black pepper, and salt (if using). Rub the seasoning all over the meat.

3. **Prepare the Vegetables:** In a large bowl, toss the mixed vegetables with olive oil, lemon juice, minced garlic, and a sprinkle of black pepper. Ensure all vegetables are evenly coated.

4. **Arrange on Baking Sheet:** Place the seasoned pork tenderloin in the center of a baking sheet or roasting pan. Arrange the mixed vegetables around the pork.

5. **Roast:** Roast in the preheated oven for about 25-30 minutes or until the pork reaches an internal temperature of 145°F (63°C) and the vegetables are tender. You can stir the vegetables halfway through for roasting.

6. **Rest and Slice:** Remove the baking sheet from the oven once cooked. Let the pork rest for about 5 minutes before slicing into medallions.

7. **Serve:** Arrange sliced pork with a generous portion of roasted vegetables on a plate. Garnish with fresh parsley if desired.

Nutritional Information (per serving): Calories: 320, Protein: 30 g, Carbohydrates: 14 g, Fats: 16 g, Fiber: 4 g, Cholesterol: 90 mg, Sodium: 260 mg, Potassium: 800 mg

- Enjoy your nutritious and satisfying meal!

Dinner: Flavorful, hearty dishes for your evening meals.

Baked Cod with Tomato Basil Relish

Prep time: 15 min	Cooking time: 20 min	Serves: 4

Ingredients

For the Cod:

4 (4-6 oz) cod fillets, skinless
1 tablespoon olive oil
½ teaspoon salt (optional)
½ teaspoon black pepper

For the Tomato Basil Relish:

2 cups cherry tomatoes, halved
¼ cup fresh basil, chopped
2 tablespoons of olive oil
1 tablespoon of balsamic vinegar
1 teaspoon garlic, minced
Salt and pepper to taste

Optional Ingredients: Lemon wedges (for serving). Additional fresh basil leaves (for garnish)

Instructions:

1. **Preheat the Oven:** Preheat your oven to 400°F (200°C).

2. **Prepare the Cod:** Place the cod fillets in a baking dish. Drizzle with 1 tablespoon of olive oil, and sprinkle with salt and pepper (if using). Ensure the cod is well coated.

3. **Prepare the Tomato Basil Relish:** In a medium bowl, combine the halved cherry tomatoes, chopped basil, 2 tablespoons of olive oil, balsamic vinegar, minced garlic, and salt and pepper to taste. Mix until well combined.

4. **Assemble the Dish:** Spoon the tomato basil relish over the cod fillets evenly, ensuring each fillet is well covered.

5. **Bake:** Place the baking dish in the preheated oven and bake for 15-20 minutes, or until the cod flakes easily with a fork and is cooked through (internal temperature of 145°F or 63°C).

6. **Serve:** Remove the baking dish from the oven once cooked. Serve the cod topped with more tomato basil relish, if desired, and garnish with additional basil leaves and lemon wedges if using.

Nutritional Information (per serving): Calories: 280, Protein: 27 g, Carbohydrates: 10 g, Fats: 16 g, Fiber: 2 g, Cholesterol: 70 mg, Sodium: 300 mg (without added salt), Potassium: 800 mg

Enjoy this nutritious and delicious meal!

Zucchini Lasagna

Prep time: 20 min	Cooking time: 35 min	Serves: 6

Ingredients

For Lasagna:

three medium zucchinis, sliced lengthwise into thin strips (about 1/8 inch thick)
1 lb. lean ground turkey or lean ground beef
2 cups marinara sauce (low sugar, no added sugar)
1 cup ricotta cheese (low-fat or part-skim)
1 cup shredded mozzarella cheese (part-skim or low-fat)
1/2 cup grated Parmesan cheese
1 small onion, finely chopped
2 cloves garlic, minced
1 teaspoon dried oregano
1 teaspoon dried basil
1/2 teaspoon black pepper
1/2 teaspoon salt (optional)

1 tablespoon olive oil

Optional Ingredients: Fresh basil leaves for garnish. Sliced mushrooms, spinach, or bell peppers (for added vegetables)

Instructions:

1. **Preheat the Oven:** Preheat your oven to 375°F (190°C).

2. **Prepare the Zucchini:** Sprinkle zucchini slices with salt and let them sit for about 10 minutes to absorb moisture. Pat dry with paper towels to remove excess moisture.

3. **Cook the Meat:** Heat olive oil over medium heat in a large skillet. Add the chopped onion and minced garlic, sautéing until softened (about 3-4 minutes). Add the ground turkey (or beef) to the skillet, cooking until browned and fully cooked, breaking it up as you stir—season with oregano, basil, black pepper, and salt (if using). Stir in the marinara sauce and simmer for a few minutes until heated through.

4. **Layer the Lasagna:** In a 9x13 inch baking dish, spread a thin layer of meat sauce on the bottom. Layer zucchini strips on top, followed by a layer of ricotta cheese and meat sauce. Repeat the layers, ending with zucchini slices on top. Spread the

remaining meat sauce over the top layer of zucchini and sprinkle with mozzarella and Parmesan cheese.

5. **Bake:** Cover the baking dish with foil (to prevent sticking; you can spray the foil with cooking spray) and bake for 25 minutes. Remove the foil and bake for 10-15 minutes or until the cheese is bubbly and golden.

6. **Cool and Serve:** Allow the lasagna to cool for 10 minutes before slicing. Garnish with fresh basil leaves if desired. Serve warm.

Nutritional Information (per serving): Calories: 290, Protein: 25 g, Carbohydrates: 12 g, Fats: 16 g, Fiber: 3 g, Cholesterol: 70 mg, Sodium: 440 mg (without added salt), Potassium: 800 mg

Enjoy this healthy, delicious, and satisfying dish!

Lentil and Vegetable Stew

Prep time: 15 min	Cooking time: 40 min	Serves: 6

Ingredients

Main Ingredients:

1 cup of dry lentils (green or brown), rinsed

1 medium onion, chopped

2 cloves garlic, minced

2 carrots, diced

2 celery stalks, diced

1 bell pepper (any color), diced

1 zucchini, diced

1 can (14.5 oz) diced tomatoes; no added salt

4 cups low-sodium vegetable broth (or water)

1 teaspoon dried thyme

1 teaspoon dried oregano

½ teaspoon cumin (optional for added flavor)

½ teaspoon black pepper

½ teaspoon salt (optional, adjust to taste)

1 tablespoon olive oil

2 cups fresh spinach (optional, added at the end)

Optional Ingredients: 1 teaspoon red pepper flakes (for spice). Fresh parsley, chopped (for garnish)

Instructions:

1. **Prepare the Ingredients:** Rinse the lentils under cold running water and set aside. Chop the onion, garlic, carrots, celery, bell pepper, and zucchini.

2. **Mix ingredients:** Heat olive oil over medium heat in a large pot. Add the chopped onion and garlic, sautéing for about 3-5 minutes until the onion is translucent.

3. **Add Vegetables:** Stir in the diced carrots, celery, bell pepper, and zucchini. Cook for an additional 5-7 minutes until the vegetables begin to soften.
4. **Combine Ingredients:** Add the rinsed lentils, diced tomatoes (with juices), broth, thyme, oregano, cumin (if using), black pepper, and salt (if using). Stir to combine.
5. **Simmer the Stew:** Bring the mixture to a boil. Reduce heat to low, cover, and let simmer for about 25-30 minutes or until the lentils are tender.
6. **Add Spinach:** If using, stir in fresh spinach during the last 5 minutes of cooking until wilted.
7. **Serve:** Ladle the stew into bowls and garnish with fresh parsley if desired.

Nutritional Information (per serving), Calories: 230, Protein: 12 g, Carbohydrates: 38 g, Fats: 5 g, Fiber: 14 g, Cholesterol: 0 mg, Sodium: 250 mg (without added salt), Potassium: 700 mg

Enjoy this healthy, hearty, and flavorful dish!

Spaghetti Squash Primavera

Prep time: 15 min	Cooking time: 45 min	Serves: 4

Ingredients

For the Spaghetti Squash:

1 medium spaghetti squash (about 3-4 lbs.)
1 tablespoon olive oil
Salt and pepper to taste

For the Primavera:

1 cup cherry tomatoes, halved
1 bell pepper (any color), sliced
1 small zucchini, sliced
1 small yellow squash, sliced
1 cup broccoli florets
2 cloves garlic, minced
1/4 teaspoon red pepper flakes (optional for spice)

1 teaspoon dried Italian herb (oregano, basil, thyme)
1/4 cup grated Parmesan cheese (optional)
Fresh basil for garnish (optional)

Instructions:

1. **Prepare Spaghetti Squash:** Preheat the oven to 400°F (200°C). Carefully cut the spaghetti squash in half lengthwise and scoop out the seeds. Brush the inside of the squash with olive oil, and sprinkle with salt and pepper. Place both halves cut side down on a baking sheet lined with parchment paper.

2. **Roast the Squash:** Bake in the oven for 30-40 minutes or until the flesh is tender and easily shredded with a fork. Remove from the oven and let cool for a few minutes before scraping the inside with a fork to create spaghetti-like strands.

3. **Prepare the Primavera:** Heat 1 tablespoon of olive oil over medium heat in a large skillet. Add the minced garlic and sauté for about 1 minute until fragrant. Add the cherry tomatoes, bell pepper, zucchini, yellow squash, and broccoli florets to the skillet. Sauté for about 5-7 minutes until the vegetables are tender but crisp.

4. **Season the Vegetables:** Stir in red pepper flakes (if using) and dried Italian herbs. Cook for another minute to heat through. Adjust seasoning with salt and pepper to taste.

5. **Combine and Serve:** Add the spaghetti squash strands to the skillet with vegetables, tossing gently to combine. If desired, sprinkle with grated Parmesan cheese. Serve warm, garnished with fresh basil if using.

Nutritional Information (per serving): Calories: 210, Protein: 8 g, Carbohydrates: 18 g, Fats: 10 g, Fiber: 6 g, Cholesterol: 3 mg, Sodium: 250 mg, Potassium: 600 mg

Enjoy this nutritious, satisfying, and delicious dish!

Lemon Herb Chicken Thighs

Prep time: 10 min   **Cooking time: 40 min**   **Serves: 4**

Ingredients

For the Chicken Thighs:

4 bone-in, skin-on chicken thighs (about 1.5 lbs.)
2 tablespoons of olive oil
Zest and juice of 1 lemon
3 cloves garlic, minced
1 teaspoon dried rosemary
1 teaspoon dried thyme
½ teaspoon black pepper
½ teaspoon salt (optional, adjust to taste)
Optional Ingredients: Fresh parsley chopped (for garnish). Lemon wedges (for serving)

Instructions:

1. **Preheat the Oven:** Preheat your oven to 400°F (200°C).

2. **Prepare the Marinade:** In a small bowl, whisk together the olive oil, lemon zest, lemon juice, minced garlic, rosemary, thyme, black pepper, and salt (if using).

3. **Marinate the Chicken:** Add the thighs in a large zip-lock bag or a shallow dish. Pour the marinade over the chicken, ensuring each piece is well coated. Allow the chicken to marinate at room temperature for about 15 minutes while the oven heats (or refrigerate for longer if preparing ahead).

4. **Arrange in Baking Dish:** Place the marinated chicken thighs skin-side up in a baking dish. Pour any remaining marinade over the chicken.

5. **Bake the Chicken:** Bake in the preheated oven for 35-40 minutes, until the internal temperature reaches 165°F (75°C) and the skin is golden and crispy.

6. **Serve:** Once cooked, remove the chicken from the oven and let it rest for 5 minutes. Garnish with fresh parsley and serve with lemon wedges if desired.

Nutritional Information (per serving): Calories: 320, Protein: 28 g, Carbohydrates: 2 g, Fats: 22 g, Fiber: 0 g, Cholesterol: 120 mg, Sodium: 300 mg (without added salt), Potassium: 500 mg

Enjoy this easy-to-prepare, flavorful, and satisfying dish!

Beef Stir-Fry with Bell Peppers

Prep time: 15 min	Cooking time: 10 min	Serves: 4

Ingredients

Main Ingredients:

1 lb. lean beef (sirloin or flank steak), thinly sliced

2 bell peppers (any color), sliced

1 medium onion, sliced

2 cups of broccoli florets

2 tablespoons low-sodium soy sauce

1 tablespoon olive oil

1 teaspoon garlic, minced

1 teaspoon ginger, minced

1 teaspoon cornstarch mixed with 1 tablespoon water (optional, for thickening)

½ teaspoon black pepper

½ teaspoon salt (optional)

Optional Ingredients: 1 tablespoon sesame oil (for added flavor), one teaspoon red pepper flakes (for heat). Chopped green onions (for garnish)

Instructions:

1. **Prepare the Ingredients:** Slice the beef against the grain into thin strips. Slice the bell peppers and onion, and cut the broccoli into florets.

2. **Make the Marinade:** In a bowl, combine the soy sauce, garlic, ginger, black pepper, and sesame oil (if using). Add the sliced beef to the marinade and let it sit for 10 minutes to absorb the flavors.

3. **Heat the Pan:** Heat the olive oil over medium-high heat in a large skillet or wok.

4. **Cook the Beef:** Using a slotted spoon, remove the beef from the marinade (reserve it) and add it to the hot skillet. Stir-fry the beef for about 3-4 minutes until it is browned and cooked to your desired doneness. Remove the meat from the skillet and set aside.

5. **Stir-Fry the Vegetables:** In the same skillet, add the sliced onion, bell peppers, and broccoli. Stir-fry for about 3-4 minutes until the vegetables are tender-crisp.

6. **Combine and Thicken:** Return the beef to the skillet with the vegetables. If you want a thicker sauce, stir in the cornstarch mixture and any reserved marinade. Stir everything together and cook for 1-2 minutes until heated through and the sauce has thickened.

7. **Serve** hot, garnished with chopped green onions if desired.

Nutritional Information (per serving): Calories: 250, Protein: 30 g, Carbohydrates: 14 g, Fats: 10 g, Fiber: 3 g, Cholesterol: 75 mg, Sodium: 480 mg (without added salt), Potassium: 750 mg

Enjoy this nutritious and satisfying meal that's quick to prepare!

Grilled Salmon with Asparagus

Prep time: 10 min   **Cooking time: 15-20 min**   **Serves: 4**

Ingredients

For Salmon:

4 (4-6 oz) salmon fillets (skin-on or skinless)
2 tablespoons of olive oil
Juice of 1 lemon

2 cloves garlic, minced
1 teaspoon dried dill or fresh dill (optional)
½ teaspoon black pepper
½ teaspoon salt (optional)

For the Asparagus:

1 lb. asparagus, trimmed
1 tablespoon olive oil
½ teaspoon garlic powder
½ teaspoon black pepper
¼ teaspoon salt (optional)

Optional Ingredients: Lemon wedges (for serving). Fresh parsley or dill for garnish

Instructions:

1. **Preheat the Grill:** Preheat your grill to medium-high heat (about 375°F to 400°F).

2. **Prepare the Marinade for Salmon:** In a small bowl, whisk together olive oil, lemon juice, minced garlic, dill, black pepper, and salt (if using).

3. **Marinate the Salmon:** Place the salmon fillets in a shallow dish or a zip-lock bag. Pour the marinade over the fillets, coating them evenly. Let the salmon marinate for 10-15 minutes while preparing the asparagus.

4. **Prepare the Asparagus:** In a mixing bowl, toss the trimmed asparagus with olive oil, garlic powder, black pepper, and salt (if using). Ensure all spears are evenly coated.

5. **Grill the Salmon and Asparagus:** Once the grill is preheated, place the salmon fillets skin-side down on the grill. Cook for 5-7 minutes per side or until the salmon flakes easily with a fork and has excellent grill marks. Add the asparagus to the grill next to the salmon, grilling for about 5-7 minutes, turning occasionally, until tender and charred.

6. **Serve:** Remove the salmon and asparagus from the grill once cooked. Serve the grilled salmon warm alongside the asparagus. Garnish with lemon wedges and fresh herbs if desired.

Nutritional Information (per serving): Calories: 350, Protein: 34 g, Carbohydrates: 8 g, Fats: 20 g, Fiber: 4 g, Cholesterol: 75 mg, Sodium: 300 mg (without added salt), Potassium: 800 mg

Enjoy your delicious Grilled salmon with asparagus!

Thai Chicken Lettuce Wraps

Prep time: 15 min	Cooking time: 10 min	Serves: 4

Ingredients

For the Chicken Filling:

1 lb. ground chicken (or ground turkey)

1 tablespoon olive oil

3 cloves garlic, minced

1 small onion, finely chopped

1 red bell pepper, diced

1 cup shredded carrots (or matchsticks)

¼ cup low-sodium soy sauce

1 tablespoon fish sauce (optional for added depth)

1 tablespoon fresh lime juice

1 teaspoon grated fresh ginger

1 tablespoon hoisin sauce (low sugar, if available)

1 teaspoon sesame oil

½ teaspoon red pepper flakes (optional for spice)

For Serving:

1 head butter lettuce or iceberg lettuce, leaves separated

¼ cup fresh cilantro, chopped (for garnish)

¼ cup chopped peanuts or cashews (optional for crunch)

Instructions:

1. **Prepare the Ingredients:** Gather and measure all the ingredients. Rinse the lettuce leaves and set aside to dry.

2. **Cook the Chicken Filling:** In a large skillet, heat the olive oil over medium heat. Add the chopped onion and minced garlic and sauté for about 2-3 minutes until fragrant and the onion is translucent.

3. **Add Vegetables and Chicken:** Add the ground chicken to the skillet, breaking it up with a spatula. Cook until the chicken is no longer pink, for about 5-7 minutes. Stir in the diced red bell pepper and shredded carrots. Cook for another 2-3 minutes until the vegetables are tender.

4. **Season the Filling:** Add the soy sauce, fish sauce (if using), lime juice, grated ginger, hoisin sauce, sesame oil, and red pepper flakes (if using). Stir well to combine and simmer for another minute to heat through and mix the flavors.

5. **Assemble the Lettuce Wraps:** Take a lettuce leaf and spoon a generous amount of the chicken filling into the center. Top with chopped cilantro and peanuts or cashews if using.

6. Serve the lettuce wraps immediately, allowing each person to assemble their own wrap. Enjoy!

Nutritional Information (per serving): Calories: 280, Protein: 28 g, Carbohydrates: 10 g, Fats: 12 g, Fiber: 3 g, Cholesterol: 85 mg, Sodium: 450 mg (without added salt), Potassium: 600 mg

Enjoy this flavorful and satisfying meal that caters to your dietary needs!

Cabbage Roll Casserole

rep time: 15 min   **Cooking time: 50 min**   **Serves: 6**

Ingredients

For the Casserole:

1 medium head of cabbage, chopped (about 4 cups)
1 lb. lean ground turkey or lean ground beef
1 small onion, diced
2 cloves garlic, minced
1 can (14.5 oz) diced tomatoes; no added salt
1 can (15 oz) tomato sauce, no added sugar
1 cup cooked brown rice or quinoa (optional; adjust carbs as needed)
1 teaspoon dried oregano
1 teaspoon dried basil
½ teaspoon paprika
½ teaspoon black pepper
½ teaspoon salt (optional)

Optional Ingredients: 1 cup shredded low-fat mozzarella cheese (for topping), 1 tablespoon Worcestershire sauce (for depth of flavor). Fresh parsley, chopped (for garnish)

Instructions:

1. **Preheat the Oven:** Preheat your oven to 350°F (175°C).

2. **Prepare the Cabbage:** Bring a large pot of water to a boil. Add the chopped cabbage and blanch for 3-4 minutes until slightly tender. Drain and set aside.

3. **Cook the Meat:** In a large skillet over medium heat, add a bit of oil if needed, then sauté the diced onion and minced garlic until tender, about 3-4 minutes. Add the ground turkey or beef to the skillet until browned and fully cooked (about 5-7 minutes). Drain excess fat if necessary.

4. **Combine Ingredients:** In a large mixing bowl, combine the cooked meat, diced tomatoes (with juices), tomato sauce, cooked rice or quinoa (if using), oregano, basil, paprika, black pepper, and salt (if using). Mix well.

5. **Assemble the Casserole:** In a greased 9x13 inch baking dish, layer half of the blanched cabbage at the bottom. Spread the meat mixture evenly over the cabbage, then top with the remaining cabbage.

6. **Add Cheese (Optional):** If desired, sprinkle shredded mozzarella cheese over the top of the casserole.

7. **Bake:** Cover the baking dish with foil and bake for 30 minutes. Remove the foil and bake for 10-15 minutes until the casserole is heated and the cheese is melted.

8. **Serve:** Allow to cool for a few minutes before serving. Garnish with chopped fresh parsley if desired.

Nutritional Information (per serving): Calories: 260, Protein: 28 g, Carbohydrates: 20 g, Fats: 10 g, Fiber: 5 g, Cholesterol: 80 mg, Sodium: 330 mg (without added salt), Potassium: 750 mg
Enjoy your hearty casserole!

Sweet Potato & Black Bean Tacos

Prep time: 15 min   **Cooking time: 30 min**   **Serves: 4**

Ingredients

For the Tacos:

2 medium sweet potatoes, peeled and diced (about 3 cups)

1 can (15 oz) black beans, rinsed and drained

1 tablespoon olive oil

1 teaspoon cumin

1 teaspoon smoked paprika

½ teaspoon chili powder

½ teaspoon garlic powder

½ teaspoon salt (optional)

½ teaspoon black pepper

8 small corn tortillas

Optional Ingredients: 1 avocado, sliced, ¼ cup feta or cotija cheese, crumbled, Fresh cilantro, chopped. Lime wedges for serving

Salsa Ingredients:

1 cup diced fresh tomatoes

¼ cup red onion, finely chopped

1 tablespoon fresh lime juice

1 tablespoon fresh cilantro, chopped

Salt and pepper to taste

Instructions:

1. **Preheat the Oven:** Preheat your oven to 400°F (200°C).

2. **Roast the Sweet Potatoes:** In a large bowl, toss the diced sweet potatoes with olive oil, cumin, smoked paprika, chili powder, garlic powder, salt, and pepper until evenly coated. Spread the sweet potatoes on a baking sheet in a single layer and roast for 25-30 minutes, turning once halfway through, until tender and slightly crispy.

3. **Prepare the Black Beans:** While the sweet potatoes roast, in a small saucepan, heat the black beans over low heat, adding a touch of water if necessary to prevent sticking—season lightly with salt and pepper to taste.

4. **Make the Salsa:** In a small bowl, combine diced tomatoes, red onion, lime juice, fresh cilantro, and a pinch of salt and pepper. Mix well and set aside.

5. **Assemble the Tacos:** Warm the corn tortillas in a dry skillet or microwave. Spoon a portion of roasted sweet potatoes into each tortilla, add black beans, and top with avocado slices, cheese, and salsa.

6. **Serve:** Garnish with fresh cilantro and serve immediately with lime wedges.

Nutritional Information (per serving): Calories: 320, Protein: 10 g, Carbohydrates: 55 g, Fats: 10 g, Fiber: 15 g, Cholesterol: 5 mg, Sodium: 380 mg, Potassium: 800 mg

Enjoy this flavorful, nutritious meal!

Baked Apples with Cinnamon with Cinnamon and Walnuts

Prep time: 15 min	Cooking time: 25 min	Serves: 4

Ingredients:

4 medium apples (such as Granny Smith or Honeycrisp)

1/2 cup chopped walnuts (optional)

1 tsp cinnamon

1/4 cup oats (preferably rolled oats for added fiber)

2 tbsp sugar substitute (like erythritol or monk fruit sweetener)

1 tbsp unsweetened almond butter (optional, adds creaminess)

1 tbsp lemon juice (to prevent browning)

1/2 cup unsweetened almond milk (or any low-carb milk)

Optional toppings: Greek yogurt (unsweetened), a sprinkle of nutmeg

Instructions:

1. **Preheat the Oven:** Preheat your oven to 350°F (175°C).
2. **Prepare the Apples:** Wash and core the apples, leaving the bottom intact (so the filling doesn't fall out). Place the cored apples in a baking dish.
3. **Make the Filling:** In a bowl, combine chopped walnuts, oats, cinnamon, sugar substitute, and lemon juice. Add the almond butter to the mixture for added creaminess and flavor. Stir until the ingredients are well combined.
4. **Stuff the Apples:** Evenly fill each apple with the walnut and oat mixture, packing it down slightly to ensure it holds together.
5. **Add Liquid:** Pour the almond milk into the bottom of the baking dish to help steam the apples and keep them moist during baking.
6. **Bake the Apples:** Cover the baking dish with aluminum foil and cook in the oven for 20 minutes. After 20 minutes, remove the foil and bake for 10-15 minutes, or until the apples are tender and the filling is golden brown.
7. **Serve:** Let the apples cool slightly before serving—top with a dollop of unsweetened Greek yogurt, if desired, for added protein and creaminess.

8. **Nutritional Information (per serving)**: Calories: 180, Protein: 4g, Carbohydrates: 25g, Fats: 8g, Fiber: 5g, Cholesterol: 0mg, Sodium: 1mg, Potassium: 250mg

Enjoy your healthy treat!

Dark Chocolate Avocado Mousse

Prep time: 10 min   **Cooking time: 10 min**   **Serves: 4**

Ingredients:

2 ripe avocados

1/4 cup unsweetened cocoa powder

1/4 cup unsweetened almond milk (or other low-carb milk)

1/4 cup sugar substitute (like erythritol or monk fruit)

1 tsp vanilla extract

Pinch of salt

Optional toppings: unsweetened whipped cream, dark chocolate shavings (sugar-free), or fresh berries

Instructions:

1. **Prepare Ingredients:** Cut the avocados in half, remove the pit, and scoop the flesh into a blender or food processor.
2. **Blend the Ingredients:** Add cocoa powder, almond milk, sugar substitute, vanilla extract, and a pinch of salt to the blender.
3. **Blend Until Smooth:** Blend on high until the mixture is creamy and smooth, scraping down the sides as necessary to ensure even blending.
4. **Taste and Adjust:** Taste the mousse and adjust the sweetness by adding more sugar substitute if desired. Blend again if needed.
5. **Chill:** Spoon the mousse into serving dishes and refrigerate for at least 30 minutes to allow it to thicken up slightly.
6. **Serve:** Serve chilled, top with optional toppings like whipped cream, chocolate shavings, or berries.

Nutritional Information (per serving): Calories: 150, Protein: 3g, Carbohydrates: 12g, Fats: 10g, Fiber: 6g, Cholesterol: 0mg, Sodium: 40mg, Potassium: 480mg

Enjoy this mousse as a dessert or a snack. Pair it with a source of protein like Greek yogurt or nuts for a balanced meal.

Cranberry Orange Sorbet

Prep time: 10 min   **Freezing time: 2-4 hours**   **Serves: 4**

Ingredients:

2 cups of fresh or frozen cranberries

1 cup of water

1/3 cup sugar substitute (like erythritol or monk fruit)

Zest of 1 medium orange

1/2 cup fresh orange juice (about 1-2 oranges)

1 tbsp lemon juice (optional for additional tartness)

Instructions:

1. **Cook the Cranberries:** In a saucepan, combine cranberries and water. Bring to a boil, reduce heat, and simmer for 10 minutes or until the cranberries have burst and softened.

2. **Sweeten the Mixture:** Remove from heat and stir in the sugar substitute, orange zest, and freshly squeezed orange juice. Optionally, add lemon juice for extra tartness. Allow the mixture to cool slightly.

3. **Blend:** Transfer the cranberry-orange mixture to a blender or food processor. Blend until smooth. Strain through a fine mesh sieve to remove solids for a smoother texture if desired.

4. **Freeze the Sorbet:** Pour the blended mixture into an airtight container and place it in the freezer. Freeze for at least 2-4 hours or until it is firm.

5. **Serve:** Before serving, let the sorbet sit at room temperature for a few minutes to soften slightly. Scoop into bowls and enjoy!

Nutritional Information (per serving): Calories: 60, Protein: 0.5g, Carbohydrates: 15g, Fats: 0g, Fiber: 2g, Cholesterol: 0mg, Sodium: 1mg, Potassium: 150mg

This Cranberry Orange Sorbet is a delightful way to enjoy a fruity treat while keeping carbohydrate and sugar levels in check!

Low-Carb Cheesecake Bites

Prep time: 15 min   Cooking time: 15 min   Chilling time: 2 hours   Serves: 12 bites

Ingredients:
For the crust:
1 cup almond flour
2 tbsp melted coconut oil or unsalted butter
1 tbsp sugar substitute (like erythritol or monk fruit)
Pinch of salt
For the cheesecake filling:
8 oz cream cheese, softened
1/2 cup Greek yogurt (plain, unsweetened)
1/4 cup sugar substitute
1 tsp vanilla extract
1 large egg

Instructions:

1. **Preheat the Oven:** Preheat your oven to 325°F (160°C).
2. **Make the Crust:** In a medium bowl, mix almond flour, melted coconut oil (or butter), sugar substitute, and salt until well combined. Press the mixture evenly into the bottom of a lined 12-cup mini muffin tin.
3. **Bake the Crust:** Bake the crust in the oven for 10-12 minutes or until lightly golden. Please remove it from the oven and cool slightly.
4. **Prepare the Cheesecake Filling:** In a mixing bowl, combine softened cream cheese, Greek yogurt, sugar substitute, vanilla extract, and egg. Beat with a hand or stand mixer on medium speed until the mixture is smooth and well combined.
5. **Fill the Crusts:** Pour the cheesecake filling evenly over the cooled crusts in the muffin tin.
6. **Bake the Cheesecake Bites:** Bake in the oven for 15 minutes or until the filling is set and slightly firm to touch.
7. **Chill:** Let the cheesecake bites cool at room temperature, then refrigerate for at least 2 hours to firm up.

8. **Serve:** Carefully remove the cheesecake bites from the muffin tin and serve chilled. Optionally, top with fresh berries or a drizzle of sugar-free chocolate sauce.

Nutritional Information (per bite): Calories: 100, Protein: 3g, Carbohydrates: 4g, Fats: 9g, Fiber: 1g, Cholesterol: 30mg, Sodium: 105mg, Potassium: 80mg

These Low-Carb Cheesecake Bites are a simple, nutritious way to satisfy your sweet tooth while maintaining a healthy diet suitable for individuals managing diabetes! Enjoy!

Coconut Macaroons

Prep time: 10 min   **Cooking time: 15 min**   **Serves: 12 macaroons**

Ingredients:

2 1/2 cups unsweetened shredded coconut

1/4 cup sugar substitute (erythritol or monk fruit)

2 large egg whites

1 tsp vanilla extract

1/4 tsp salt

Optional: 1/4 cup sugar-free chocolate chips for dipping or drizzling

Instructions:

1. **Preheat the Oven:** Preheat your oven to 325°F (160°C). Line a baking sheet with parchment paper.

2. **Mix the Ingredients:** In a large mixing bowl, combine the shredded coconut, sugar substitute, egg whites, vanilla extract, and salt. Mix thoroughly until all the coconut is well moistened and holding together.

3. **Shape the Macaroons:** Using your hands or a small cookie scoop, form small mounds or balls (about 1-2 tablespoons each) and place them onto the prepared baking sheet, spacing them about 1 inch apart.

4. **Bake:** Bake in the oven for 12-15 minutes or until the tops are golden brown. Keep an eye on them to prevent burning.

5. **Cool:** Remove from the oven and let the macaroons cool on the baking sheet for a few minutes before transferring them to a wire rack to cool completely.

6. **Optional Chocolate Drizzle:** If desired, melt sugar-free chocolate chips in the microwave or a double boiler. Drizzle over the cooled macaroons for added flavor.

Nutritional Information (per macaroon): Calories: 90, Protein: 1g, Carbohydrates: 5g, Fats: 7g, Fiber: 2g, Cholesterol: 0mg, Sodium: 30mg, Potassium: 70mg

These Coconut Macaroons are easy to prepare and provide a nutritious and satisfying option for those managing diabetes without compromising on taste! Enjoy!

Sugar - Free Pumpkin Pie

Prep time: 15 min   **Cooking time: 50 min**   **Serves: 8**

Ingredients:

For the crust:
1 1/2 cups of almond flour
1/4 cup coconut oil or unsalted butter, melted
2 tbsp sugar substitute (erythritol or monk fruit)
1/2 tsp salt
1 large egg

For the filling:
1 can (15 oz) pure pumpkin puree (not pumpkin pie filling)
3 large eggs
1 cup unsweetened almond milk (or other low-carb milk)
1/2 cup sugar substitute (like erythritol or monk fruit)
1 tsp vanilla extract
1 tsp ground cinnamon
1/2 tsp ground nutmeg
1/4 tsp ground ginger
1/4 tsp salt

Instructions:
1. **Preheat the Oven:** Preheat your oven to 350°F (175°C).
2. **Make the Crust:** In a mixing bowl, combine almond flour, melted coconut oil (or butter), sugar substitute, salt, and egg. Mix until the dough forms. Press the crust mixture into a 9-inch pie pan evenly across the bottom and sides. Prick the bottom with a fork to prevent bubbling.
3. **Pre-bake the Crust:** Bake the crust in the oven for 10-12 minutes or until slightly golden. Remove from the oven and set aside to cool slightly.

4. **Prepare the Filling:** In a large bowl, whisk together the pumpkin puree, eggs, almond milk, sugar substitute, vanilla extract, cinnamon, nutmeg, ginger, and salt until smooth and well combined.
5. **Fill the Crust:** Pour the pumpkin filling into the pre-baked almond flour crust, spreading it evenly.
6. **Bake the Pie:** Bake in the oven for 35-40 minutes, or until the pie is set and the center is firm. You can check doneness by inserting a knife in the center; it should come out clean.
7. **Cool:** Allow the pie to cool on a wire rack for at least 30 minutes before slicing. For best results, chill in the refrigerator for another hour before serving.

Nutritional Information (per slice): Calories: 140, Protein: 4g, Carbohydrates: 9g, Fats: 10g, Fiber: 3g, Cholesterol: 70mg, Sodium: 150mg, Potassium: 200mg

This Sugar-Free Pumpkin Pie is a delightful, healthy option for fall or any time of year, providing a tasty, sweet treat while maintaining a diabetic-friendly profile. Enjoy!

Zucchini Brownies

Prep time: 15 min	Cooking time: 30 min	Serves: 12 brownies

Ingredients:

1 cup finely grated zucchini (about one medium zucchini)

1/2 cup unsweetened almond butter (or peanut butter)

1/4 cup sugar substitute (erythritol or monk fruit)

1/4 cup unsweetened cocoa powder

2 large eggs

1 tsp vanilla extract

1/2 tsp baking soda

1/2 tsp baking powder

1/4 tsp salt

Optional: 1/2 cup sugar-free chocolate chips or chopped nuts for added texture

Instructions:

1. **Preheat the Oven:** Preheat your oven to 350°F (175°C). Line an 8x8-inch baking dish with parchment paper or lightly grease it.
2. **Prepare the Zucchini:** Grate it and press it in a clean paper towel or cheesecloth to remove excess moisture. This ensures the brownies aren't too wet.
3. **Mix Wet Ingredients:** In a large mixing bowl, combine the almond butter, sugar substitute, eggs, and vanilla extract. Mix until smooth.
4. **Add Dry Ingredients:** To the wet mixture, add the grated zucchini, cocoa powder, baking soda, baking powder, and salt. Stir until everything is well combined.

5. **Add Optional Ingredients:** Fold the sugar-free chocolate chips or nuts into the batter for added flavor and texture.
6. **Pour into Baking Dish:** Pour the batter into the prepared baking dish and spread it evenly with a spatula.
7. **Bake:** Bake in the preheated oven for 20-25 minutes, or until a toothpick inserted in the center comes out clean or with a few moist crumbs. Avoid overbaking to keep the brownies moist.
8. **Cool:** Allow the brownies to cool in the pan for about 10-15 minutes, then lift out using the parchment paper and let them cool completely on a wire rack before cutting into squares.

Nutritional Information (per brownie): Calories: 120, Protein: 4g, Carbohydrates: 10g, Fats: 8g, Fiber: 2g, Cholesterol: 0mg, Sodium: 100mg, Potassium: 150mg

These Zucchini Brownies provide a scrumptious and healthy option that caters to the dietary needs of individuals managing diabetes while still satisfying your sweet tooth. Enjoy!

Lemon Gelatin Dessert

Prep time: 10 min　　　　**Chilling time: 2 hours**　　　　**Serves: 4**

Ingredients:

1 package (0.3 oz) sugar-free lemon gelatin (such as Jell-O brand)
1 cup of boiling water
1 cup unsweetened almond milk (or other low-carb milk)
1/2 cup fresh lemon juice (about 2-3 medium lemons)
Optional: 1-2 tbsp sugar substitute (erythritol or monk fruit) to taste
Optional garnish: fresh lemon slices or berries

Instructions:

1. **Dissolve the Gelatin:** In a mixing bowl, dissolve the sugar-free lemon gelatin in 1 cup of boiling water. Stir until fully dissolved.

2. **Add Liquid Ingredients:** Stir 1 cup of unsweetened almond milk and 1/2 cup of freshly squeezed lemon juice. If desired, add a sugar substitute to taste for extra sweetness.

3. **Mix Thoroughly:** Ensure everything is well mixed. Taste the mixture and adjust sweetness if necessary.

4. **Pour into Molds:** Pour the gelatin mixture into individual serving cups or a mold of your choice.

5. **Chill:** Refrigerate the gelatin dessert for at least 2 hours or until it is firm and set.

6. **Serve:** Once set, serve chilled. Optionally, garnish with fresh lemon slices or a few berries for an appealing presentation.

Nutritional Information (per serving): Calories: 25, Protein: 1g, Carbohydrates: 2g, Fats: 1g, Fiber: 0g, Cholesterol: 0mg, Sodium: 30mg, Potassium: 70mg

This easy-to-make Lemon Gelatin Dessert is a delicious, healthy option for those managing diabetes while enjoying a sweet treat! Enjoy!

Chocolate Dipped Strawberries

Prep time: 10 min   **Cooking time: 30 min**   **Serves: 12 strawberries**

Ingredients:

12 fresh strawberries (preferably medium to large)

1/2 cup sugar-free dark chocolate chips (look for options with 70% cocoa or higher)

1 tsp coconut oil (optional for a smoother melt)

Optional toppings: crushed nuts, unsweetened shredded coconut, or a sprinkle of sea salt

Instructions:

1. **Prepare Strawberries:** Wash the strawberries thoroughly and pat them dry with a paper towel. Ensure they are completely dry, as water can prevent the chocolate from adhering.

2. **Melt the Chocolate:** Combine the sugar-free dark chocolate chips and optional coconut oil in a microwave-safe bowl. Microwave in 20-30-second intervals, stirring after each interval, until the chocolate is fully melted and smooth.

3. **Dip the Strawberries:** Hold a strawberry by the stem and dip it into the melted chocolate, swirling to coat about two-thirds of the strawberry. Allow any excess chocolate to drip off.

4. **Add Toppings (Optional):** If desired, immediately sprinkle your chosen toppings (crushed nuts, shredded coconut, or sea salt) on the chocolate-covered strawberries before the chocolate hardens.

5. **Chill the Strawberries:** Place the dipped strawberries on a parchment-lined baking sheet. Refrigerate for about 30 minutes or until the chocolate is set and firm.

6. **Serve:** Once the chocolate is set, serve the chocolate-dipped strawberries on a decorative plate as a delicious and healthy dessert.

Nutritional Information (per chocolate-dipped strawberry): Calories: 50, Protein: 1g, Carbohydrates: 8g, Fats: 3g, Fiber: 1g, Cholesterol: 0mg, Sodium: 1mg, Potassium: 150mg

Enjoy this delightful and healthy treat that caters to diabetes patients while enjoying delicious flavors!

Diabetic-Friendly Peanut Butter Cookies

Prep time: 10 min   **Cooking time: 10-12 min**   **Serves: 12 cookies**

Ingredients:

1 cup natural peanut butter (unsweetened, no added sugar)

1/4 cup sugar substitute (like erythritol or monk fruit)

1 large egg

1 teaspoon vanilla extract

1/4 teaspoon baking soda

1/4 teaspoon salt

Optional: 1/4 cup sugar-free chocolate chips or chopped nuts for added texture

Instructions:

1. **Preheat the Oven:** Preheat your oven to 350°F (175°C). Line a baking sheet with parchment paper.

2. **Mix Ingredients:** In a mixing bowl, combine the peanut butter, sugar substitute, egg, vanilla extract, baking soda, and salt. Mix until the dough is smooth and well combined.

3. **Add Optional Ingredients:** Add sugar-free chocolate chips or nuts to the dough for added flavor and texture.

4. **Shape the Cookies:** Using a tablespoon or cookie scoop, a spoonful of dough onto the prepared baking sheet, spacing them about 2 inches apart. Flatten each cookie slightly with the back of a fork, creating a crisscross pattern.

5. **Bake:** Bake in the oven for 10-12 minutes or until the edges are golden. The cookies will firm up as they cool.

6. **Cool:** Allow the cookies to cool on the baking sheet for 5 minutes before transferring them to a wire rack to cool completely.

Nutritional Information (per cookie): Calories: 110, Protein: 4g, Carbohydrates: 5g, Fats: 9g, Fiber: 1g, Cholesterol: 15mg, Sodium: 60mg, Potassium: 150mg

These Diabetic-Friendly Peanut Butter Cookies are delicious, easy to make, and cater to those managing diabetes while satisfying your sweet cravings! Enjoy!

Chapter 4: Bonus Section

Here is a 30-day diabetic-friendly meal plan focusing on balanced, nutritious meals that are low in sugar and carbohydrates and rich in protein and fiber.

Day 1

Breakfast: Scrambled eggs with spinach and tomatoes

Lunch: Grilled chicken salad with mixed greens and vinaigrette

Dinner: Baked salmon with steamed broccoli

Snack: Celery sticks with peanut butter

Day 2

Breakfast: Greek yogurt with berries and a sprinkle of cinnamon

Lunch: Turkey lettuce wraps with avocado

Dinner: Stir-fried tofu with vegetables

Snack: A small apple with almond butter

Day 3

    Breakfast: Oatmeal made with unsweetened almond milk, topped with walnuts

    Lunch: Quinoa salad with cucumber, bell peppers, and feta

    Dinner: Grilled shrimp with zucchini noodles

    Snack: Baby carrots with hummus

Day 4

    Breakfast: Chia seed pudding made with almond milk and topped with berries

    Lunch: Tuna salad with leafy greens and olives

    Dinner: Roasted chicken thighs with Brussels sprouts

    Snack: A handful of mixed nuts

Day 5

    Breakfast: Smoothie with spinach, protein powder, and unsweetened almond milk

    Lunch: Lentil soup with a side salad

    Dinner: Baked cod with asparagus

    Snack: Greek yogurt

Day 6

    Breakfast: Cottage cheese with sliced strawberries

    Lunch: Grilled vegetable wrap using a whole-grain tortilla

    Dinner: Turkey meatballs with spaghetti squash

    Snack: Sliced cucumber with tzatziki sauce

Day 7

    Breakfast: Omelet with bell peppers and onions

    Lunch: Chickpea salad with tomatoes, parsley, and lemon dressing

    Dinner: Grilled flank steak with roasted cauliflower

    Snack: Handful of almonds

Day 8

    Breakfast: Smoothie with kale, protein powder, and almond milk

    Lunch: Baked chicken breast with quinoa and steamed green beans

Dinner: Stir-fried shrimp with snow peas and bell peppers

Snack: String cheese

Day 9

Breakfast: Greek yogurt mixed with chia seeds and a few berries

Lunch: Spinach salad with hard-boiled eggs and avocado

Dinner: Zucchini boats stuffed with ground turkey

Snack: Celery sticks with almond butter

Day 10

Breakfast: Scrambled eggs with cottage cheese and herbs

Lunch: Veggie and bean chili

Dinner: Grilled pork chops with sautéed spinach

Snack: A small pear

Day 11

Breakfast: Oatmeal with ground flaxseeds and cinnamon

Lunch: Lentil and vegetable stew

Dinner: Baked salmon with quinoa and asparagus

Snack: A few slices of red bell pepper with hummus

Day 12

Breakfast: Egg and avocado on whole-grain toast

Lunch: Quinoa salad with black beans and corn

Dinner: Grilled chicken with roasted sweet potatoes

Snack: A small serving of mixed nuts

Day 13

Breakfast: Smoothie with spinach, almond milk, and a scoop of protein

Lunch: Grilled chicken Caesar salad (light dressing)

Dinner: Beef stir-fry with broccoli

Snack: Greek yogurt

Day 14

Breakfast: Chia seed pudding with almond milk and berries

Lunch: Turkey and cheese roll-ups with lettuce

Dinner: Vegetable curry with lentils

Snack: A handful of walnuts

Day 15

Breakfast: Scrambled eggs with salsa and avocado

Lunch: Spinach and walnut salad

Dinner: Baked tilapia with mixed vegetables

Snack: Sliced cucumber with guacamole

Day 16

Breakfast: Smoothie with kale, avocado, and protein powder

Lunch: Quinoa and chickpea salad

Dinner: Grilled chicken thighs with roasted Brussels sprouts

Snack: A small apple with nut butter

Day 17

Breakfast: Cottage cheese with berries

Lunch: Grilled chicken with a mixed greens salad and vinaigrette

Dinner: Zucchini noodles topped with marinara sauce and turkey meatballs

Snack: A small handful of almonds

Day 18

Breakfast: Greek yogurt smoothie with spinach and a few berries

Lunch: Egg salad in lettuce cups

Dinner: Baked chicken with roasted cauliflower

Snack: Baby carrots with hummus

Day 19

Breakfast: Overnight oats with chia seeds and almond milk

Lunch: Lentil soup with spinach

Dinner: Grilled shrimp skewers with vegetable stir-fry

Snack: A few slices of bell pepper with tzatziki

Day 20

Breakfast: Scrambled eggs with diced tomatoes and avocado

Lunch: Quinoa salad with cucumbers, olives, and feta

Dinner: Beef and broccoli stir-fry

Snack: Greek yogurt topped with a few walnuts

Day 21

Breakfast: Omelet with mushrooms and cheese

Lunch: Spinach salad with grilled chicken and light dressing

Dinner: Stuffed bell peppers with ground turkey and quinoa

Snack: A small pear or apple

Day 22

Breakfast: Smoothie with kale, protein powder, and unsweetened almond milk

Lunch: Turkey and avocado lettuce wraps

Dinner: Baked cod with sautéed spinach

Snack: Celery sticks with peanut butter

Day 23

Breakfast: Greek yogurt with sliced almonds and cinnamon

Lunch: Chickpea salad with cherry tomatoes and parsley

Dinner: Grilled chicken breast with quinoa and zucchini

Snack: Handful of mixed nuts

Day 24

Breakfast: Egg muffins with spinach and cheese

Lunch: Tuna salad stuffed avocado

Dinner: Beef stew with carrots and celery

Snack: A few slices of cucumber with hummus

Day 25

Breakfast: Chia seed pudding made with almond milk

Lunch: Grilled vegetable wrap in a whole-grain tortilla

Dinner: Shrimp tacos in lettuce wraps

Snack: String cheese

Day 26

Breakfast: Smoothie with almond milk, spinach, and protein powder

Lunch: Lentil and vegetable soup

Dinner: Grilled flank steak with roasted sweet potatoes

Snack: A small apple with almond butter

Day 27

Breakfast: Overnight oats with chia seeds and berries

Lunch: Spinach salad with feta and walnuts

Dinner: Zucchini lasagna

Snack: Sliced bell peppers with tzatziki

Day 28

Breakfast: Omelet with bell peppers and onions

Lunch: Turkey and cheese roll-ups with a side salad

Dinner: Baked salmon with asparagus

Snack: Greek yogurt with a sprinkle of cinnamon

Day 29

Breakfast: Cottage cheese with sliced strawberries

Lunch: Grilled chicken salad with avocado and nuts

Dinner: Stir-fried tofu with mixed vegetables

Snack: Handful of walnuts

Day 30

Breakfast: Scrambled eggs with salsa and avocado

Lunch: Quinoa and chickpea salad

Dinner: Roasted chicken thighs with Brussels sprouts

Snack: Celery sticks with hummus

Notes:

Adjust Portions: Tailor portion sizes based on individual calorie and carbohydrate needs.

Stay Hydrated: Drink plenty of water throughout the day.

Snacks: Choose snacks high in protein or fiber to help stabilize blood sugar levels.

Sugar Substitutes: Use diabetic-friendly sweeteners (like erythritol or stevia) for recipes or drinks when necessary.

Meal Prep: Prepare meals in advance where possible to help make healthy choices easier.

This 30-day meal plan is designed to provide a variety of nutritious, delicious foods that support a healthy lifestyle for individuals managing diabetes while still enjoying a range of flavors!

Chapter 5: Final Thoughts & Encouragement

As you close this book, I hope you feel empowered, excited, and ready to create. Cooking with diabetes in mind may seem challenging, but it's a journey that rewards you with newfound creativity and deeper awareness of your body's needs. Each recipe in these pages was crafted to inspire you to embrace flavor, nourishment, and variety without compromise.

Remember, your kitchen is a place of joy and innovation. It's where ingredients are transformed, and health meets taste in the most delightful ways. While you may start with the recipes here, the real magic happens when you adapt, experiment, and make these dishes your own. Trust your instincts, play with spices, and cherish the process as much as the outcome.

Life with diabetes is not defined by limits but by choices that you have the power to make every day. Let this cookbook be a companion that encourages you to make those choices confidently and excitedly. Celebrate every small success, share your creations with loved ones, and savor each bite as a reminder of your dedication to wellness.

Thank you for allowing these recipes to be part of your journey. Here's to meals that are not only diabetic-friendly but life-friendly—where food is as much about health as happiness. You're not just cooking; you're creating moments, memories, and a future full of delicious possibilities.

To your health and happiness,

Tori Jones.

Made in the USA
Coppell, TX
15 December 2024

42642297R00044